"NOTHING REAL
CAN BE THREATENED"
Exploring A Course In Miracles

Other books by Tara Singh

HOW TO LEARN FROM A COURSE IN MIRACLES

THE FUTURE OF MANKIND

AWAKENING A CHILD FROM WITHIN

COMMENTARIES ON A COURSE IN MIRACLES

A GIFT FOR ALL MANKIND

"LOVE HOLDS NO GRIEVANCES" –
THE ENDING OF ATTACK

DIALOGUES ON A COURSE IN MIRACLES

HOW TO RAISE A CHILD OF GOD

THE VOICE THAT PRECEDES THOUGHT

REMEMBERING GOD IN EVERYTHING YOU SEE

"WHAT IS THE CHRIST?"

MOMENTS OUTSIDE OF TIME

"NOTHING REAL CAN BE THREATENED"

Exploring A Course In Miracles

TARA SINGH

LIFE ACTION PRESS
Los Angeles

Library of Congress Cataloging-in-Publication Data
Singh, Tara, 1919-
Nothing real can be threatened:
exploring A course in miracles / Tara Singh.
ISBN 1-55531-240-3 (alk. paper): $24.95
ISBN 1-55531-230-6 (pbk.: alk. paper): $13.95
1. Foundation for Inner Peace. Course in miracles.
2. Fear – Religious aspects.
3. Peace of mind – Religious aspects.
4. Spiritual life. 5. New Age movement. I. Title.
BP605.N48F68 Suppl. 9   89-35821
299'.93–dc20   CIP

10 9 8 7 6 5 4

The ideas represented herein are the personal interpretation and
understanding of the author and have not been endorsed by the
copyright holder of *A Course in Miracles*.

Quotations from *A Course in Miracles* ©1975, 1992,
and *The Gifts of God* ©1982, are reprinted by permission
of the copyright holder, the
Foundation for Inner Peace,
P.O. Box 1104, Glen Ellen, California 95442.

Printed on acid-free paper.

*I am most grateful for the many friends
who have made this book possible:
Lucille Frappier, Howard and Bette Schneider,
Charles Johnson, Aliana Scurlock, Jim Cheatham,
Frank Nader, Clio Dixon, Susan Berry,
Jim Walters, and Barbara Dunlap.*

CONTENTS

page

INTRODUCTION   *11*

1   THERE ARE NO PROBLEMS
    APART FROM THE MIND   *31*

2   "NOTHING REAL CAN BE THREATENED"   *41*

3   FREEDOM FROM FEAR   *57*

4   LETTING GO IS THE ISSUE —
    DISCUSSIONS ON FEAR   *75*

5   FEAR IS NOT A REALITY   *103*

6   INDIVIDUALITY   *123*

7   ULTIMATELY
    WE HAVE TO CONQUER FEAR   *135*

page

8   THE NEED TO STEP OUT OF THOUGHT   *159*

9   THOUGHT IS INSANITY   *171*

10 THE PRESSURES ON MANKIND   *185*

11 "I CAN BE HURT BY NOTHING
     BUT MY THOUGHTS"   *197*

12 "I AM UNDER NO LAWS BUT GOD'S" —
     A COMMENTARY   *209*

     "THE DREAM OF FEAR"   *235*

ADDENDA

     AUTOBIOGRAPHY OF TARA SINGH   *243*

     THE PURPOSE OF THE
     FOUNDATION FOR LIFE ACTION   *263*

     STATEMENT OF THE PARTICIPANTS
     OF THE ONE YEAR
     NON-COMMERCIALIZED RETREAT   *267*

     REFERENCES   *269*

     OTHER MATERIALS BY TARA SINGH
     RELATED TO A COURSE IN MIRACLES   *279*

SAFETY

The wish to harm alone engenders fear.
Without it is protection obvious,
And shelter offered everywhere. There is
No time when safety need be sought, no place
Where it is absent, and no circumstance
Which can endanger it in any way.
It is secured by every loving thought,
Made more apparent by each loving glance,
Brought nearer by forgiving words, and kept
Untroubled, cloudless, open to the light,
Redeemed, restored and holy in Christ's sight.

This poem is from *The Gifts Of God* by Helen Schucman, the Scribe of *A Course In Miracles* (Foundation for Inner Peace, 1982), page 8. It is an incomparable book of poetry containing some of the most important words ever spoken.

INTRODUCTION

OUR STORY — AN EXTENSION OF "NOTHING REAL CAN BE THREATENED"

WHEN I WAS INTRODUCED to *A Course In Miracles*,[1] its impact made all else secondary forever. An involuntary action within me introduced a new order, brought my heart to gladness, and provided the space to discover whether it was possible to apply:

Nothing real can be threatened.
Nothing unreal exists.[2]

I spent one hundred days with the Course in spacious aloneness. The practice of each day's lesson brought my mind to the remembrance of true words and the sacredness that accompanied them became my most precious treasure. If I forgot to repeat the lesson, the Course reassured me:

You will probably miss several applications, and perhaps quite a number. Do not be disturbed by this, but do try to keep on your schedule from then on.[3]

The inspiration of this freed me from all sense of guilt and punishment. There are no consequences — hence, in reality, no reaction. What an astonishing discovery: truth unfolds like a flower within the mind emptied of itself! The duality of punishment and reward, on which society is based, begins to crumble before your very eyes. Even the vanity of the loveless "I know and you don't" slowly starts to fall away. A new vitality, the inner conviction of your own reality, emerges — a clarity that begins to dispel thousands of years of misbelief.

You wonder why you had never questioned the obvious falseness of separation and of one's own opinion. The tragedy is that one's opinions are not even one's own. I was astonished. How could I have walked half a century in my life so oblivious of being a second-hand human being? Partial attention motivates meaningless activity. Ever-seeking in my isolation, it exhausted me. All we *know* is what we have borrowed or what has been imposed upon us. Our thoughts are mere assumptions, for the most part. There is no love, no peace, no truth, no gratefulness outside of the Mind of God.

Now I began to see the realm of my own thought as wholly false. Attachment to the things of the world loosened its grip and, at the same time, thoughtfulness and gratefulness spontaneously began extending themselves.

This transformation had its own divine way of unfolding. It was an awakening of impersonal intelligence that sees the world of ideas as meaningless and the world of nature with calm eyes. Out of this stillness emerges the recognition of man's function on earth.

What a joy it is for the Son of God to know that he has never wronged, that he is forever impeccable. This liberated me from my own opinions and I began to step out of the dream world of illusion.

Each lesson of *A Course In Miracles* brings one to a contact with reality. This is the miracle Jesus offers those who earnestly yearn for salvation, for He is ...*in charge of the process of Atonement.*[4] I was amazed and grateful to know how effortless the process of awakening is.

When the capacity to receive flowers, one has something of one's own to give. This transformation is what each lesson of *A Course In Miracles* makes possible. The blessing of the Course is the energy of love it imparts for you to share with your brother. What a joy to discover that the dwelling place of the Holy Spirit is in holy relationship. The holy relationship is the temple of God.

> *The holy instant is the Holy Spirit's most useful learning device for teaching you love's meaning. For its purpose is to suspend judgment entirely.*[5]

> *The holy relationship is the expression of the holy instant in living in this world. Like everything about salvation, the holy instant is a practical device, witnessed to by its results. The holy instant never fails. The experience of*

it is always felt. Yet without expression it is not remembered. The holy relationship is a constant reminder of the experience in which the relationship became what it is. And as the unholy relationship is a continuing hymn of hate in praise of its maker, so is the holy relationship a happy song of praise to the Redeemer of relationships.[6]

The Course teaches you to turn your problems over to the Holy Spirit. But man denies the ability of the Holy Spirit to dissolve his problems because to turn them over demands recognition of what the Holy Spirit's function really is. It is the call for help itself that relates one with the Holy Spirit — and you discover the problems are dissolved even before you formulate your inadequacy. It is the power of your *little willingness*[7] that invites the Action of Grace into your life.

And now gratefulness surrounds you. It, too, is absolute and outside of time. It relates you with the Divine Intelligence of Eternal Laws. Gratefulness is not just the sentimentality of "thank you." Thought came into being after the separation and cannot understand the benediction of gratefulness.

I was told directly:

INGRATITUDE IS THE ONLY SIN.

("Sin" means separation.) Ingratitude is self-destructive. Seeking sensation and gratification, it binds one to the illusions of the body senses. Ingratitude exploits and abuses everything and everyone with its self-interest. It is the denial of the Action of Grace, and prevents the correction of misperception.

After the hundred days of quietude, and the realization of,

> *Nothing real can be threatened.*
> *Nothing unreal exists.*

a new action of non-commercialized life began for the first time in the history of the New World. This action to help the earnest student bring *A Course In Miracles* into application took the form of the One Year Non-Commercialized Retreat: A Serious Study of *A Course In Miracles.* The retreat took place in Los Angeles, California, from Easter Sunday, April 3, 1983, to Easter Sunday, April 22, 1984. It was an historic event, this day-by-day study of the Course without any charge of tuition.

Before the One Year Retreat, the Foundation for Life Action* was earning nearly $1,000 a day from workshops and retreats, and the sale of books and tapes. But any interest in making money was finished. Now, with fear and insecurity gone, and having something of one's own to give, the action unfolded in this way.

We discovered that the undoing of unwillingness is essential. All else is of secondary importance. Even though there may be eagerness to learn, learning can

---

* The Foundation for Life Action, which sponsored the One Year Retreat, is a federally approved, nonprofit, educational foundation founded by Tara Singh in 1980. (Editor)

become an indulgence, a deception when left to the activity of the brain — which it usually is. We discovered that understanding is verbal and merely a shift of opinion, and that feelings and enthusiasm are short-lived. Unless one realizes, as an actuality, that there is resistance to internal change, miracles, and holy instants, the blocks the ego continues to evade remain.

The knowledge of ideas is the knowledge of "about," and must be perceived as meaningless. Only the true student can say:

I am determined to see things differently.[8]

Without conviction, it is not possible to dissolve the illusions of time and live by holy relationship.

We discovered that ingratitude is the characteristic of the non-student. Ingratitude is equivalent to unwillingness. It is distrust of goodness. The ungrateful cannot recognize the ingratitude within their own lives.

A non-student lacks faith; it is his defense against change. Defenses are fearful. Yet, vulnerability is essential, for in reality there is nothing to lose or be threatened by. What is real is never threatened by the externals. Since ingratitude cannot correct itself, it distrusts the teacher. And once reverence is lost, there is not the teacher-student relationship.

Where the relationship is one-to-one and life-for-life, the integrity of the student is of primary importance from the very outset. It requires great discrimination on the part of the teacher, even though it be lacking in the student. The non-student evades the challenge life presents and misses out. He cannot step out of the past.

Authentic teachers have been few and far between throughout the centuries. And true students, amongst those who are self-convinced that they are very serious, are rare exceptions as well. Words have lost their meaning where man believes in whatever he projects.

We discovered that WHAT IS GOOD IS BAD ALSO.

Affluence is "good" to the brain, the seat of sensation and gratification. It is "good" for today's commercialized lifestyle and the sale of violence. But its "good" is questionable when wisdom is lost, simplicity gone, and disharmony rampant. In overly externalized life, even relationships have become mere expediences.

We have discovered that very few realize the vitality of awareness. Awareness is a state of being in which there is no interpretation, nor time. It transmits the creative energy of eternity and effects a change equivalent to rebirth. "Having the ears to hear"[9] brings one to full attention where the Given is received and instantly in application. It is an awakening in which neither effort nor personality is involved. Transformation is instantaneous. This is how swiftly the Holy Spirit, or the teacher of God, corrects misperception.

But ultimately, the foremost discovery we made was how strong and deceptive is the inherent unwillingness in man to change.

THE EGO MAKES SURE
NEVER TO FIND WHAT IT SEEKS.[10]

Yet, knowing the difficulties of coming to the truth of:

> *Nothing real can be threatened.*
> *Nothing unreal exists.*

as well as wanting a meaningful life, twenty people stayed in Los Angeles at the end of the One-Year Retreat, inspired by:

"There must be another way."[11]

The Foundation for Life Action introduced those who stayed to the strength of rightness and a different lifestyle, and provided a conducive atmosphere for them to come to self-reliance, intrinsic work, productive life, and having something of their own to give.

It was felt that once the external pressures were removed, they would have a better chance of bringing the Course into application. But in our present economic system it is difficult to come to self-reliance without determination. We witnessed that the difficulties are almost insurmountable. Self-reliance comes to men and women who have developed professional skills, who have awakened their capacities to be reliable, factual, and competent without being competitive. Their integrity and devotion to their undertaking will not allow another, nor indulgence, to intrude upon their space.

We began to discover that self-reliance is a step outside the values of the world. It demands, *I will not value what is valueless.*[12] We were blessed to see that it was by working together with Eternal Laws that we could learn the true meaning of intrinsic work that leads to self-reliance. This whole action emerged out of:

> *Nothing real can be threatened.*
> *Nothing unreal exists.*

We discovered that man, in his isolation, can project ideas and pursue success, but the wise is never caught in the pursuit of accomplishment. Free of expectation, he is never disappointed. Mr. J. Krishnamurti[13] said,

> "Wisdom has no direction."

Accomplishment is contrary to perfection — which already exists, knows no lack, and projects no plans.

These are earth-shaking truths, difficult to comprehend or to bring into application. But to each one of the twenty, the Foundation for Life Action became a place where one sensed a Presence that was always there and kept us renewed. Even things we would normally have resistance to doing, we cherished. Without the Action of Grace, the harmony would never have been possible.

It is the gratefulness for the gift of *A Course In Miracles*, as well as the opportunity provided by the

Foundation, that leads the group towards the One Mind. The Foundation never charged for its services and included those who came, in its action of extending the values of the Course. The Foundation is ever to adhere to the principle of never owning property so as not to become a householder. Domesticity has its obligations by which one is controlled.

During our fifth year together, we decided to amicably disband, since we still were not getting past the intellectual level of understanding the Course. Things had improved at the external level, but the Foundation is strictly a school devoted to internal transformation. No one at the Foundation wanted to go out and teach mere words that they had learned from another, words which were born out of their interpretation. They refused to go out and interpret a truth that was not theirs.

I spoke with Kenneth Wapnick, a man with an authentic voice, and said that we were closing the doors after five years, adding, "Can you believe it? Not one of them feels capable to go out and teach the Course." He said, "That speaks of their humility. And it also speaks of you, their teacher, who inspired that, and did not mislead them with false enthusiasm of who they are."

We all agreed to leave. There were no attachments — either to the world or to the Foundation. It was a surprise that we could disband like the Essenes.[14] They were the only ones known in history to have done so. It is most difficult to voluntarily end anything. We talked things over openly, as always, and decided that we would disband in spite of things going well at the personal level.

I decided to do a benefit retreat[15] so that each one could leave with some money. But after the retreat they did not want to touch a single penny of the proceeds, saying, "You have given us your life. We are grateful for what has been imparted to us. How can we accept the money?" So that brings the highest goodness on both sides.

There once was a great king in ancient India, Yudhishthira of the *Mahabharata*,[16] who never told a lie. Being detached, he would always first reject anything offered to him. Then, if he wanted to accept it, he did so on his own terms. Now that they had passed the test of not being attached, I asked, "What would you really like to do?" Unanimously, the group voiced their desire to stay and continue their meaningful work. With this came a new energy.

On April 2, 1989, the ending of the sixth year, the most amazing thing happened. A small group came forward to take the next step — from understanding, at the idea level, to internally realizing the truth of:

I am sustained by the Love of God.[17]

I am the Light of the world.
That is my only function.
That is why I am here.[18]

There is no peace except the peace of God.[19]

This is the text of the statement they signed and presented to me.

* * * * *

I SEEK A FUTURE
DIFFERENT FROM THE PAST[20]

What meaning would our lives have had
without the sacredness of *A Course In Miracles*
that energizes us with every lesson?

With grateful hearts
we give thanks to our teacher, as well,
for our transformed values and productive lives.
We were lost without him.

He gives of himself totally
and reveals to us that goodness is whole and of God.
It can never be sold, only shared.

Now, before a lit altar, we have taken an oath
to work amongst ourselves as One Mind,
knowing no lack, and honoring:

LOVE YE ONE ANOTHER.[21]

Ours is a commitment to:

SEEK YE FIRST THE KINGDOM OF GOD,
AND HIS RIGHTEOUSNESS;
AND ALL THINGS
SHALL BE ADDED UNTO YOU.[22]

We have been blessed by the six and more years
of one-to-one relationship,
hardly conceivable in present society.
Yet it exists, irrespective of external values —

neither limited to, nor destroyed by, commercialism.
Nothing in the world would have merited
the rightness of this action in our lives.

As we now go out two-by-two to share,
it is our decision to give our whole mind and heart
to the sacredness of *A Course In Miracles*
and to our direct experience of self-reliance.

We are energized by the action of self-giving
and the potential to actualize it.
The ability to overcome self-interest
is being awakened.

Self-interest is the basic issue.
The brain is now in charge
and will not let go the experiencing of sensation.
But total attention is the fire
that dissolves the illusion of "becoming."

We have seen that without having
the capacity to listen,
it is not possible to realize the Truth of:

> *Nothing real can be threatened.*
> *Nothing unreal exists.*

Our going out is not to offer solutions,
but to arouse an energy of pure sensitivity
to the Course and right action in life.

What a joy to dedicate our lives
to seeing the living Christ in our brother.
Our action, born of awareness, is:

LIFE FOR LIFE.

* * * * *

Those who are at the Foundation for Life Action are not necessarily the students of the School at *The Branching of the Road*,[23] but they have agreed to make things possible for the true students who may come. By so doing, some may well emerge as students themselves.

The group at the Foundation is now getting on its own feet. This frees me, and out of the given space, emerges Joseph's Plan.[24] No greater gift have I ever received than this boon of selfless life. It allows me to live free of motive as a guest upon the planet.

Out of desirelessness, man's real work begins as he realizes it is service that is productive. There is no greater joy for a man than a life enriched by service. He will neither sell himself nor the Name of God. The action that originates out of stillness slowly begins to restore the mind to innocence. One recalls the words of Lord Krishna:

> "I have no duties to perform,
> yet I engage in action."[25]

Each person who comes to realize:

> *To give and to receive are one in truth,*[26]

would have to define in his own words the state that is an extension of fulfillment. The definition of that state would be ever new, not of borrowed phraseology, and therefore, no one in collective consciousness would likely accept it. Jesus would have the same difficulty communicating with the multitude. The clergy that restates second-hand language is popular and prosperous. But it is instantaneous newness that makes the Given accessible.

The action of Joseph's Plan begins with the Forty Days in the Wilderness Retreat, the awakening in America of New Intelligence, consistent with the spirit of the Forefathers —

"IN GOD WE TRUST."[27]

Proceeds from the Forty Days Retreat are to be set aside and given exclusively to meet man's primary needs in times to come.

Joseph's Plan is impersonal and holy. And only those who have outgrown self-interest and are self-reliant can qualify to be an extension of it.

Joseph's Plan demonstrates to the world THERE IS NO LACK. It is the renewal of the Spirit of Divine Intelligence amongst the few in the world who are selfless. Our discovery is that motiveless life is impersonal and has its own vitality, blessings, and direct guidance. Joseph's Plan is an involuntary response to human need. And blessed are those who merit and become part of it.

With Joseph's Plan come new challenges. At the relative level, it is almost impossible for thought not to interfere with direct response to human need. Thought, itself being reaction, remains ignorant of a state that knows no lack. With Joseph's Plan, insight enters our relative world of duality with its own wisdom.

At the Foundation for Life Action, we insist on bringing insights and holy instants into application. To do this one has to be free of interpretation and the fear of consequences. This is the expression of a life that is non-personal. These are the astonishing changes which miracles and insights have brought about in our minds and hearts at the Foundation:

We no longer have opposing views, nor expect any situation to be different than it is. Changing one situation for another, we have discovered, does not make the inner correction. Finding fault in the external is an irresponsibility that evades correction within. The direct contact with "what is" begins to release us from choices, preferences, and the conflict to which a personalized life is subject.

This means that we must never overlook the fact that man, as God created him, is perfect. We must make a correction in our own misperception. Perhaps this awareness, in itself, could communicate the vision of wholeness which acknowledges no sense of limitation, nor problem, as real.

The challenge of not recognizing a problem as a fact imparts a strength that awakens potentials of higher levels within. But for the most part, present society lives at the relative level where there are problems. In the search for solutions, we usually evade the problems by escaping into the sub-level of indulgences. Endless distractions are provided in deeply-conditioned modern society, where hardly anyone has his own mind.

Joseph's Plan is a direct response that by-passes the brain and its relative thought system. What freedom not to have an opposing view about any situation. WHAT IS, IS. The vision of it ends conflict and any sense of inadequacy. How could we deny that the Force which multiplied the fish and the bread[28] is still active in the world?

There is an Action of Grace that is independent, having its own intelligence. It is the very source of creation. Its power is not of the earth. Self-reliance, or non-commercialized action, or having something of one's own to give have to be directly related to this divine energy for them to be real.

The purpose of this book is to introduce you, the reader, to the Action of Life that discovers and extends the truth of:

> *Nothing real can be threatened.*
> *Nothing unreal exists.*

The energy that extends
Nothing real can be threatened
flows like a river of life-giving water and light
that nourishes and illuminates the mind of the age.

At the Foundation for Life Action,
the Given is made accessible.

Tara Singh
May 17, 1989
Angel Fire, New Mexico

CHAPTER ONE

"Creation's gentleness is all I see."

I have indeed misunderstood the world, because I laid my sins on it and saw them looking back at me. How fierce they seemed! And how deceived was I to think that what I feared was in the world, instead of in my mind alone. Today I see the world in the celestial gentleness with which creation shines. There is no fear in it. Let no appearance of my sins obscure the light of Heaven shining on the world. What is reflected there is in God's Mind. The images I see reflect my thoughts. Yet is my mind at one with God's. And so I can perceive creation's gentleness.

"In quiet would I look upon the world, which but reflects Your Thoughts, and mine as well. Let me remember that they are the same, and I will see creation's gentleness."

A Course In Miracles
Workbook For Students
Lesson 265, page 418

1

THERE ARE NO PROBLEMS APART FROM THE MIND

ALL RELIGIONS have stressed the importance of "know thyself." Throughout the ages, the wise have asked and endeavoured to discover: "Who am I?" Obviously, if one knew, one would neither ask nor explore. Yet very few have ever questioned the validity of thought itself as the means to discovery.

It is important for us to see that the relative thought by which we live is not related to reality. It is incapable of knowing the truth of "love" or what is "good," these absolute words that have no opposite.

A Course In Miracles discriminates between two thought systems. The first is the absolute thought system of God, which is love and truth. The man who lives in accord with the Thoughts of God lives by grace and is whole. His life is an extension of Timeless Laws in the world of time.

In contrast, there is the relative thought system of man by which the ego-self lives in the insanity of separation, ruled by its projected images. It is a thought system that lives, for the most part, by the energy of conflict and friction.

The major difference between the two is that the first one, knowing no lack, gives; the second, unfulfilled, ever wants.

> There are only two thought systems, and you demonstrate that you believe one or the other is true all the time.[1]

The language of the Course conveys the clarity of True Knowledge. Lesson 45 tells us:

> Under all the senseless thoughts and mad ideas with which you have cluttered up your mind are the thoughts that you thought with God in the beginning.... They will always be in your mind, exactly as they always were. Everything you have thought since then will change, but the foundation on which it rests is wholly changeless.[2]

The Thought of God, or True Knowledge — that which is absolute — is already there and it is impersonal. What is required is the ending of one's preoccupation with the unreal world of personal thought. But the Course also makes it clear — and this clarity is of the utmost value to the student — that the ego's guiding principle is:

> Seek and do not find.[3]

The realization of this one truth cuts time and protects one from a lifetime of false pursuits.

Lesson 22 of the *Workbook For Students* deals with the intricacies of our relative thought system.

What I see is a form of vengeance.

Today's idea accurately describes the way any- one who holds attack thoughts in his mind must see the world. Having projected his anger onto the world, he sees vengeance about to strike at him. His own attack is thus perceived as self defense. This becomes an increasingly vicious circle until he is willing to change how he sees. Otherwise, thoughts of attack and counter-attack will preoccupy him and people his entire world. What peace of mind is possible to him then?

It is from this savage fantasy that you want to escape. Is it not joyous news to hear that it is not real? Is it not a happy discovery to find that you can escape? You made what you would destroy; everything that you hate and would attack and kill. All that you fear does not exist.[4]

Not unless we question thinking itself will it ever be undone. Obviously, this would result in the un- doing of our beliefs and concepts.

...the essential thing is learning that you do not know.... Yet all that stands between you and the power of God in you is but your learning of the false... Be willing, then, for all of it to be undone, and be glad that you are not bound to it forever.[5]

How easy it is to doubt; how difficult it is to have faith. Be attentive and observe closely how difficult it is to be generous or kind to yourself, and how easy it is to be wasteful. Observe how difficult it is to be trusting and not calculate. Isolated as we are — victimized by our loneliness and insecurity — sanity is nearly impossible.

Is it possible to be secure while unfulfillment is given validity? Behold how we validate unfulfillment, insecurity, and fear. Are these not the source of our attack thoughts?

> How can I know who I am when I see myself
> as under constant attack? Pain, illness, loss,
> age and death seem to threaten me. All my
> hopes and wishes and plans appear to be at the
> mercy of a world I cannot control. Yet perfect
> security and complete fulfillment are my
> inheritance. I have tried to give my inheritance
> away in exchange for the world I see.[6]

And wanting the "opposite" of the world we see is made into a goal or an ideal. The future is made real and the illusion of time enters in. Conflict will continue as long as we project and pursue the "opposite."

I am sustained by the Love of God.[7]

As an idea this is of no significance. But what would one give to know the truth of it?

Will we ever outgrow unfulfillment? Will we ever come to a state that knows no lack? Intellectuality is of no help. Its understanding does not bring about transformation. Self-preoccupation is false because our very identity is false.

We live by the insanity of the manmade world and its thought system. And although the Course offers the sanity of *God's Plan for Salvation*[8] that brings with it transformation and change of values, we are drawn to it only as an ideal, not as a fact.

But the Course reassures us:

Truth will correct all errors in my mind.[9]

It has been my experience that the student is energized by ending the preoccupation of deception. The one who is not a student, but thinks he wants to *become* a student, is attached to the illusion of learning. The difference is that one values undoing while the other is still interested in self-improvement and is going contrary to the very premise of the Course.

Undoing is arduous for the non-student. We constantly evade it, even while reading the Course. Yet all that is required is "having the ears to hear."

> *Only your misperceptions stand in your way...."Many are called but few are chosen" should be, "All are called but few choose to listen." Therefore, they do not choose right.... Right minds can do this now, and they will find rest unto their souls.*[10]

The Course, if we give it the purity of attention, brings all of this to our awareness and the illusions are undone spontaneously. There is no effort in it. One is totally free for an instant, and that instant is part of eternity also.

This gift of clarity that ends duality is the gift of God to His Son. In:

I am as God created me,[11]

there is nothing to fear. Peace is the peace of God. There is no lack in it.

Some time after I had spent four years on the Himalayas as an ascetic, I met Mr. J. Krishnamurti for the first time. I was stunned for weeks by what I heard him say:

"THERE ARE NO PROBLEMS
APART FROM THE MIND."

One truth can totally revolutionize a life.

There is nothing in the world that could pay for the blessing of an involuntary, creative moment. The wise person would give everything he owns for a few minutes in the presence of a man whose words are realized.

In ancient times, the relationship between the teacher and the student was one-to-one, life-for-life, and non-commercial. The sages imparted True Knowledge that transformed the student. They did not so much teach as transmit the light of truth. The true teacher needed to say something only once. The student, "having the ears to hear," inherited the energy of the Word, and thus never became dependent on the teacher.

It is such reverence for True Knowledge that brings about a right relationship between the student and *A Course In Miracles.*

We need to adhere to the daily practice of the lesson, not as a duty, but as a means of stepping out of the preoccupation of the brain and making contact with the eternity of our own being. It will correct all errors, change our values, and cut time.

> *Be very still an instant. Come without all thought of what you learned before, and put aside all images you made. The old will fall away before the new without your opposition or intent.*[12]

You will see a new order come into being and discover how precious is spacious aloneness. Your own stillness will introduce you to peace within yourself. For,

> *When you are still an instant, when the world recedes from you, when valueless ideas cease to have value in your restless mind, then you will hear His Voice. So poignantly He calls to you that you will not resist Him longer. In that instant He will take you to His home, and you will stay with Him in perfect stillness, silent and at peace, beyond all words, untouched by fear and doubt, sublimely certain that you are at home.*[13]

CHAPTER TWO

"All fear is past and only love is here."

All fear is past, because its source is gone, and all its thoughts gone with it. Love remains the only present state, whose Source is here forever and forever. Can the world seem bright and clear and safe and welcoming, with all my past mistakes oppressing it, and showing me distorted forms of fear? Yet in the present love is obvious, and its effects apparent. All the world shines in reflection of its holy light, and I perceive a world forgiven at last.

"Father, let not Your holy world escape my sight today. Nor let my ears be deaf to all the hymns of gratitude the world is singing underneath the sounds of fear. There is a real world which the present holds safe from all past mistakes. And I would see only this world before my eyes today."

A Course In Miracles
Workbook For Students
Lesson 293, page 435

2

"NOTHING REAL CAN BE THREATENED"

EVERYTHING IN CREATION emerges out of light. In its origin creation is light. It can be called the light of love or the energy of creation or the vibration of energy. But in reality, behind appearances, there is only the absolute and it is the source of all things.

As creation begins to activate and manifest, prana comes into being. Prana is pure energy. Then air comes into being, followed by water and finally solidified matter.

In order to understand what thought is, we have to recognize that thought itself has substance and that it came into being after the separation took place. In wholeness there is no thought. In the purity of silence there is no thought. Silence, ever attentive and energetic, is a fire. We carry the light within. But it requires attention to *be* of the light.

What is of thought is limited. Being partial, it lacks honesty. Because thought is subject to the duality of cause and effect it cannot know totality. It does, however, serve an important purpose: while thought cannot enter silence, it can touch upon silence.

It is in the silent mind where conflict ends, and True Knowledge — the Given — is accessible. In every sentence of the Course, if one is willing to give the attention that makes the space, there are miracles that introduce one to the Absolute Word, the Source of creation.

The Mind the Course speaks of with a capital "M" is the Mind of God, the One Mind we all share. True Knowledge is of this state of wholeness where there are no levels, and all is one.

Thought, obviously, is of the human brain, hence personal and time bound. It is possible for man to outgrow thought, but it requires questioning every idea and belief, every dogma and concept that limits us to our thought system.

And what is the content of the "knowings" of thought? For the most part, is it not doubt and fear, desire and sorrow, insecurity and lack, judgment and ambition? The first response of thought is always fear; it is forever suspicious and limited to the plane of duality. It is always this versus that, you and me, good and bad, love and hate, big and small, and so on. Can thought know that which is measureless and has no "opposite"?

By seeing its limitations, however, we can use thought to transcend thought. This requires integrity. When thought is rightly used, it sees its own limitation because it touches upon another, purer energy — the silent energy of awareness.

Silence is supreme. It knows no separation, no "opposite"; it is whole and holy. Out of silence is born a different intelligence. Although thought cannot enter silence, it has served its purpose of bringing you there. The right use of intelligence is to realize the limitation of the relative thought system by which we live.

Although thought is involuntary and cannot be controlled, the still mind, seeing the deception of how thought splits itself and opposes what it wants, can end the activity of thought.

Very few, however, have been able to break through the duality of the thinking process. We stay at the level of effort. Our understanding is of thought and therefore, does not go very far. When thought "understands" something, it is always because it sees in it something advantageous. Because thought does not know fulfillment, it always has a lack and, consequently, seeks to identify with pleasure, status, or success. Are we not thought-led individuals who live a lifestyle of conflict and unfulfillment?

And now to us has been given *A Course In Miracles* to bring us to the realization of our relationship with the eternal. Is one who is related to the eternal ever under pressure? Would he need outlets and distractions? His is a life of ethics and self-mastery, of virtue and goodness, of compassion and thoughtfulness. Because he has order in his life, he can come to the

One Mind of which we are all a part — the Mind of God.

Unless that separation has ended in each one of us, there is nothing but the struggle of thought and ideas, and each one continues to remain separated. Inherent in the separation of a "you" and a "me," there will always be fear, conflict, and insecurity.

A Course In Miracles has come to end that separation and to dissolve misperception.

> *Nothing real can be threatened.*

These are perhaps the strongest words ever spoken upon the planet. The light of truth is in them.

Have you ever come to a clarity within yourself that is beyond the known? The preoccupation of our knowing seldom allows us the space to discover the new, which is timeless. Now that we have the Course, what is required is the capacity to receive. The Action of Grace accompanies those who make space for the Voice of the Course.

> *...grace cannot come until the mind prepares itself for true acceptance. Grace becomes inevitable instantly in those who have prepared a table where it can be gently laid and willingly received.... we prepare for grace in that an open mind can hear the Call to waken. It is not shut tight against God's Voice. It has become aware that there are things it does not know, and thus is ready to accept a state completely different*

from experience with which it is familiarly at home.[1]

The challenge is our attachment to so-called advantages. Yet only insanity would see unfulfillment as an advantage. The Course offers miracles — instants of insight to undo our illusions.

A Course In Miracles shows us why:

Nothing real can be threatened.

To question what constitutes threat is wise. Only by so doing can it be dissolved. Is it not important to free the mind from fear so that it can function efficiently?

An energetic mind has the capacity to question. It finds the light of its own awareness far superior to thought. Now internal transformation and correction begins, and relationship with the Course becomes of first importance. One's heart is filled with gratefulness as the meaningless world of self-projected images begins to disappear.

> *This is the day when vain imaginings part like a curtain, to reveal what lies beyond them. Now is what is really there made visible, while all the shadows which appeared to hide it merely sink away…. And in His judgment will a world unfold in perfect innocence before your eyes. Now will you see it with the eyes of Christ. Now is its transformation clear to you.*[2]

This is a gigantic step in which you die to the old. It is not for the passive. It seeks to achieve nothing and it needs no effort, but it requires discrimination

45

to see the false as the false. Here the very seeing dissolves the unreal. If you are totally with that, you can no longer be part of thought that is threatened.

The serious student of *A Course In Miracles* discovers the vitality of the holy instant that liberates him from misperception. Reality is never threatened. It is only thought that is threatened.

Will you question your thought system, having seen that it is constantly threatened by what is unreal? Start with yourself. Question the thoughts you trust, and discover that they are mere opinions. Now does that require effort? It may be new — but the fact is, we are unwilling to let go of the known. Are not fear and insecurity of the known? Loss and gain, achievement and failure, these too must be questioned.

Anything that is outside our memory, we do not trust. And there is a dread in us of the eternal, the Source, the Unknown that sustains, and is Life. Yet Love is the Law and the energy of creation, ever extending its completeness. The Course stresses that:

> *All the help you can accept will be provided,*
> *and not one need you have will not be met.*[3]

Finally, each of us will have to come to say, "I no longer trust in fear." There is no love without trust. And no one is religious without having dissolved the illusion of fear.

Spirit, ever uncontaminated by insecurity and the survival instinct, knows neither limitation nor death. But we have confined our existence to the body senses and the limitations of personality. For the most part, that is all we have known. Thus the known has become our bondage.

Mr. J. Krishnamurti, the light of this age, said:

> "Wisdom has no direction."

These are words perhaps never uttered before. He also said:

> "Freedom is at the beginning,
> and not at the end."

Freedom is outside of time.

If you start wherever you are with the Course, you will discover that the Holy Spirit accompanies you, and the purity of your attention will endow you with miracles.

The purpose of the Course is to bring man to his God-given function. To realize True Knowledge, the student must rise to the state of the Course and meet it. He must recognize from the very outset that the unlearning of the conventional thought system is of first importance.

I am determined to see things differently.[4]

This brings the student of the Course to the actual reversal of the thought system. *Nothing real can be threatened* means that one must reverse his thinking in order to be free of fear.

How few ever become aware that they have lost their real function in life, limited as they are to the body senses and dragged into conventional living where Eternal Laws are not valued. In the absence of knowing our function and the potentials to fulfill it, our lives result in contradiction and insoluble conflict. We can know no peace as long as the truth of our own being is violated. How quickly we indoctrinate the child with our own fears and insecurity. Then, in school, he is molded against his own nature to a meaningless life, subject to a job.

My only function is the one God gave me.[5]

The question is: what constitutes a function? It would have to be consistent with Divine Laws and thus, automatically, manmade rules would oppose it. He who *extends* is part of the creative Action of Life. Those who oppose are part of reaction. We live in a world where action always appears to be met with reaction.

Inherent in man must be the potential and the ability to fulfill his particular function. But will our educational system allow the child to discover the specific abilities with which he was born, or give him the space to realize:

Salvation is my only function here?[6]

Throughout history, the few who had discrimination made contact with eternal gratefulness, and flowered. But the goodness and gratefulness that transformed their lives were absolute. They were not learned, but realized.

Not being subject to time, the Self-realized leave behind their light and holiness, for these extend beyond the external world of appearances. Action is an extension of divine perfection. The man of Action, who has realized his Identity and is consistent with the Will of God, does not enter into psychological commotion but learns to relate with the physical world directly.

The Course introduces the student to the potentials within himself to fulfill the function that he was born to extend. As he discovers, *Light and joy and peace abide in me,*[7] he is transformed by his own holiness, and his function sets him free from the external world of appearances.

Salvation is my only function here.[8]

The true purpose of man on earth is salvation. Yet with what outrageous means have we perverted each new generation. The media and our educational systems could well be the sources of the ever-expanding violence in society. How difficult has "know thyself" become, now that we are schooled with nationalistic values. Quickly, we are trained to be subject to the authority of the externals.

What inner strength and integrity it would take to break through the bondage of one's conditioning and declare:

I will not value what is valueless.[9]

Society has seldom ever accepted one who lives by the strength of his own honesty, who does not justify his existence by being preoccupied with the valueless. The world of images and illusions, of fear and motives, rules the day. Hardly anyone is his own person. Despite what we may think, we are, for the most part, compelled and conditioned toward self-destruction.

We live in a world where almost everything we do has consequences, and our solutions are usually worse than the problems. Judgment and punishment are rampant in a world devoid of the heightened sensitivity of compassion.

Even so, most people today are somewhat tolerant of objective thought or True Knowledge — our revenge and fear are directed towards nations far away. But as the economy becomes disturbed and chaotic forces replace politics, insanity will rear its head within nations against those who do not conform. Concentration of power is already in the hands of the few.*

The challenge now is not in wanting or becoming, but in discovering how much you have to undo in order to make the space within to recognize your own untarnished holiness. No one who reads the Course need undermine himself, nor doubt the grace of God. There is nothing to learn, but there is much to unlearn. In meeting this challenge, the joy of inner correction will take place within you.

---

* For further discussion, see "The Future Of Mankind" in *The Future Of Mankind — The Branching Of The Road* by Tara Singh (Foundation for Life Action, 1986), pages 5-19. (Editor)

Each one who has yearned for day-by-day guidance now has the Course to help him realize the God-given function he came to extend. It is the true words of the Course that transform one's life and enable him to say, with words that time cannot affect:

My only function is the one God gave me.[10]

When you recognize the truth of this, you are awakened within. The action is internal.

At the time level, there is only "becoming," or learning. These evade the creative and energetic action of the present. Are not "trying" and saying, "I am going to do my best," external to the reality of the living moment? The holy instant takes place when this is understood.

> *In the holy instant it is understood that the past is gone.... The stillness and the peace of now enfold you in perfect gentleness. Everything is gone except the truth.*[11]

A Course In Miracles is the thought system of God. Because it is absolute, it has the power to transform. Every sentence endows the reader with miracles. Blessed are its lessons, and blessed are the moments the student spends with it. The mere remembrance of:

Nothing real can be threatened

energizes one. Realizing its truth, no circumstances can beguile or take one over. The wise person is not involved in fear, but observes its workings until awareness intensifies and eliminates the spell of fear.

The Course states:

God is the Light in which I see.[12]

The wise, whose knowledge is direct, sees how the world and its consequences of cause and effect have deceived mankind throughout the ages. He sees the world's attempts to make real the unreal.

What wisdom there is in learning directly how the insanity of thought dissipates one's energy. Fear is a projection of thought, and it is based on the idea of tomorrow's consequences. It is not real. The fact is, the present is protected and remains untouched by the regret of yesterday and the fear of tomorrow.

We are talking about projected, psychological fear with its consequences, not the natural fear of danger, such as that of being bitten by a rattlesnake.

To be with "what is" demands the energy and attention of the present. The passivity of partial attention will not dissolve projected fear. Being in the present overcomes fear; there is no other way. Those who are to be amongst the teachers of God[13] extend the present. For them, *There is nothing to fear.*[14] For them:

Nothing real can be threatened.
Nothing unreal exists.

This is the true strength of a state that is liberated. Merely reading the scriptures, or strengthening a belief system and being self-convinced, will not release the body senses from fear.

A Course In Miracles is different from other scriptures in that it offers step-by-step instructions and awakens latent potentials. Also, it starts with dissolving the unreality of personal opinions and false assumptions. Can we see that undoing is an essential step because we are so heavily conditioned?

The Course is a serious undertaking; it has to be lived. Miracles take place only when corrections are made. The Course introduces the earnest student to the order of Eternal Laws that sustain existence. The Son of God is a part of the Mind of God, and his reality is not limited to the training of the brain or to the body senses.

Holy are those, who by giving attention to each lesson of the day, bring their brain to its own rhythm. It is they who read the Course as if God's Voice is speaking to them.

The manmade world of the brain is in disarray and is ever in crisis. But every lesson of the Course brings order to the brain. Thus, it becomes rested, direct and energetic, untouched by resistance, and free of problems. Having its own rhythm and the heightened sensitivity of open space, the brain can now be fully attentive to an immense stillness that makes it receptive to the peace of God.

What a lesson constitutes is far beyond our knowing. Each lesson assigns its own practice, and its miracles bring True Knowledge to remembrance. A miracle is a breakthrough, the light that dispels the unreality of thought images.

To spend quiet time with the Course, morning and evening, is essential. It relaxes the brain, widens the gaps between the thoughts, cleanses the blood of toxins, and purifies the brain. Reading the Course slowly is a holy undertaking. Can you see each lesson as a boon — an Action of Grace?

The earnest student comes to the decision:

I am determined to see things differently.[15]

How few have ever made a decision in their lives, a decision that will not be swayed by choice and preference. To be a serious student of the Course requires integrity, discrimination, and a deep sense of responsibility. But miracles and holy instants will open the way.

CHAPTER THREE

I have said you have but two emotions, love and fear. One is changeless but continually exchanged, being offered by the eternal to the eternal. In this exchange it is extended, for it increases as it is given. The other has many forms, for the content of individual illusions differs greatly. Yet they have one thing in common; they are all insane. They are made of sights that are not seen, and sounds that are not heard. They make up a private world that cannot be shared. For they are meaningful only to their maker, and so they have no meaning at all. In this world their maker moves alone, for only he perceives them.

A Course In Miracles
Text
pages 230-231

3

FREEDOM FROM FEAR

IT IS EASY TO TALK ABOUT LOVE because we think love is a good thing. We already have a bias about it. And therefore, talking *about* love and preaching love is very profitable. But we can talk about it and not know what love actually is.

Many centuries have passed since the Master said, "LOVE YE ONE ANOTHER."[1] Have we learned it? We have been taught this from childhood, but try to bring it into application and you will encounter difficulty. Talking about love is not love, for only application of truth is true. Talking *about* it is not.

A Course In Miracles says in love there is no fear. And, I would suggest, nothing can free us from fear but love. We may think that other values or opinions can free us, or that there are things we can *do* to get rid of fear. We may think money can free us, or that armaments can. Yet each of these is merely an extension of fear. Why would any nation want armaments if it were not afraid? Today the whole human race is caught up in that frenzy. It has become a disease world-wide.

It is essential for us to understand what freedom from fear implies. The universities and colleges have not helped us to be free. They have trained us to run corporations and wars. What have these to do with love and freedom? Henry David Thoreau said:

> "Freedom is freedom from self. It cannot be bestowed by an institution upon a human being."

Throughout the ages people have given us definitions of love and fear, and of freedom, but what has changed? We are still insecure and afraid. These subjects demand that we be genuinely interested. Partial attention will never bring one to honesty; conflict will never know freedom; and belief systems will continue to separate man from man.

To be free from self, one has to look at what the self is. We are afraid, insecure, and filled with beliefs — and do we not also think we are helpless and guilty sinners as well? The vested interests that rule us will make sure we keep on believing this, too. How heavy a burden we carry with our belief systems and fears and insecurities! What but honesty will dissolve it?

Honesty is essential. It is not possible to be free of fear without honesty, for it is an action that dispels all that is unessential. Can we see how difficult a task that is — to be honest? As the Course points out:

...the ego never looks on what it does with perfect honesty.[2]

We can talk about honesty, and preach honesty, too. Like love, honesty is a good thing. No one would disagree with that. But in actuality, what is honesty? That is quite a question. Inevitably, we have some conclusion or idea of what honesty is, yet are ideas ever honest? We also can admit what we feel, but are feelings honest? Feelings are physical and personal, of the emotions and sensation.

There is only one brain in the world. Jealousy is jealousy everywhere. Fear is fear everywhere. In understanding ourselves, we can understand everyone because we have the same brain. Any person who sincerely wants to discover freedom from fear will have to question, "How did fear ever come into me?" The challenge is first to face it in oneself.

A Course In Miracles states:

> *The closer you come to the ego's thought system, the darker and more obscure becomes the way. Yet even the little spark in your mind is enough to lighten it. Bring this light fearlessly with you, and bravely hold it up to the foundation of the ego's thought system. Be willing to judge it with perfect honesty. Open the dark cornerstone of terror on which it rests, and bring it out into the light. There you will see that...everything of which you have been afraid was based on nothing.*[3]

Fear might be an illusion or it might be a fact, but please do not just accept someone else's words. You must discover for yourself *directly* what fear is. Preaching and teaching have failed. They have not brought peace to man, nor freedom from fear. It does not matter how many PhD's we have, conflict is still inherent in us, as is an active sense of lack. Whether you are illiterate or well educated, whether you are rich or you are poor, fear is still fear. And to be free from fear is quite an issue.

We need to really ask in a deep way: "What is insecurity?" "What is an idea?" "What is thought itself?" Are we willing to question all of these things? We must, for in the questioning is the vitality for discovery. To question is to arouse another potential within. It is quite different from accepting another's opinion. That is conformity and it is all too easy. We love being told and therefore, we deprive ourselves of the vitality of discovering our own vast potentials. And when conformity comes in, beliefs and dogmas appear.

We must value truth above all else. We could ask, "What would love be?" "What is freedom?" How few know the truth of these! A person who is capable of dissolving his own words cannot be deceived. You cannot tell such a person what truth — the absolute without opposites — is, without knowing the fact of it. He does not accept nice phrases or intellectual understanding. And neither should you.

Honesty brings illusions to light and frees you from them. It is not Christian or Buddhist, Islamic or

Jewish. Honesty is whole. There is no division in it. And it brings us to truth — that state that knows no conflict.

Now, are we willing to bring illusions to honesty in order to be free of them? There is no other way. That is quite a challenge, isn't it? Honesty goes far beyond how we feel and what we think.

Can we simply begin by questioning? Then we are already somewhat independent, because we are no longer depending on other people's words. We are all capable of making our own discoveries but we underestimate ourselves. Why is it that we evade discovering our own potentials, thinking someone else will tell us? We are evading our own reality. See how we have become more and more dependent — on other people, on books, on jobs. When you are dependent on something you give it authority over you.

In the end, we will say that we have known affluence and education, but we still cannot afford to be honest. Yet without honesty there is no freedom from fear. We must confront ourselves. A man who has love in his heart would demand honesty of his brother as well as of himself. You are capable of discovering honesty if you really want to. It is not difficult but it does require interest, attention, and internal space.

So then, what is honesty? Honesty is eternal. Honesty is free of all ideas, for it is consistent with the Will of God. Honesty is not personal. Neither is freedom personal. Can anyone personalize life? Life is of God; you and I did not invent it. And Life is One. In the One Life there is relationship, not dependence. In the One Life, how can there be fear?

The Course defines honesty thus:

> [Honesty] ...*actually means consistency. There is nothing you say that contradicts what you think or do; no thought opposes any other thought; no act belies your word; and no word lacks agreement with another. Such are the truly honest. At no level are they in conflict with themselves. Therefore it is impossible for them to be in conflict with anyone or anything.*[4]

We see that honesty is consistency at all levels of our being. When we are consistent at all levels of our being, there is no conflict. And when there is no conflict, there is vitality, integrity, and a conviction that cannot be touched by abstract fears.

But we, for the most part, live a very partial life. Only a few levels of our being are active. And when we are not whole, there is fear. There is no way to step out of it, no matter what the preacher or the guru says. As long as there is not the consistency at all levels in a human being, he will be afraid and therefore, manipulated into one belief system or another. This cannot be disputed.

Another factor of fear is lack of trust in one's own holiness, in one's own goodness, in one's own eternity. We feel helpless, and out of helplessness, fear is born. However, to be free we have to realize the truth of who we really are.

Honesty is a state independent of relative knowledge. It ends conflict and duality. It ends the verbal, and introduces us to the reality of our own being that is not subject to anything external. That would be freedom, wouldn't it? What else would you call freedom? If it is subject to circumstances and the externals, could it be free?

Freedom from fear is freedom from the externals. It is freedom from dependence. It is also freedom from time itself, with all its pressures.

Do you still want to be free, or are you now more afraid of freedom than ever? Who wants to be free? We are used to our fears, and are not bothered by the falseness of our lives.

Throughout the ages mankind has lived in societies based on expedience and dependence. In that, there is no freedom. What we have known is the energy of friction, not the energy of love. We are actually afraid of freedom. And where there is fear, there is unfulfillment and we seek outlets. Do you realize how many outlets there are in an affluent society? The very pressure of life demands them.

Yet, *A Course In Miracles* assures us:

All fear is past and only love is here.[5]

Can you imagine what a human being would be like who is untouched by fear? If all fear is past, then we are responsible for tormenting ourselves with the projections of fear: insecurity, unfulfillment, blaming another, and so on. How could we know that "love is here"?

We have to truthfully ask ourselves if we are *really* interested in freedom from fear. If we are, we will not fit into present society. And yet, can you imagine, it is society that needs the man who is free. The man who is free makes the greatest of contributions because where there is freedom, there also is love.

A person who extends freedom can be quite a threat to those who are attached to their vested interests. This has been so throughout the ages. Such a person is not caught in thought or opinion — his own or that of another. He moves from fact to fact.

Those beings who were free from fear were unique and almost always represented a threat to society. Let us examine one such example, Socrates, the flower of the civilization of Greece at its very height. Socrates was free — free from fear.

Freedom is a state of being. When you are free from fear, you are also free from personality. It is revolutionary. And each person has the potential within himself to come to that state. It is not an idea; it is not an opinion; it is not words. It is the actuality in which all levels of your being become consistent and you are charged with vitality. It has its own majesty, its own holiness. It is never assertive. It threatens no one — yet threatens the whole world. The Greek civilization shivered before a man who was free.

How this took place is very interesting. This God-lit man did not deviate from God-consciousness. He was in a different state. But the Divine Forces wanted to get him into Action. One day, a friend of Socrates went to the Temple of Delphi, where the oracle spoke, and asked the priestess if there was anyone wiser than Socrates? She replied there was no one wiser than Socrates. His friend returned and told Socrates what the oracle had said.[6]

Then one wonders: How would Socrates respond? Socrates knew the oracle to be true, but a person who is God-lit is not subject to curiosity. He does not want to know anything of relative knowledge that does not relate to truth. What would an enlightened being then say? What would such a great and virtuous person then do?

Do we have the time for that kind of pause in our lives? Perhaps that pause is a moment of freedom. Can we afford that? Can we ever stop and step out of time? Walt Whitman said, "I am as if disembodied of materiality." Have you ever had that moment, "disembodied of materiality"? That means stepping out. That is the moment of freedom.

We are so afraid, we do not allow ourselves the space or the time. We do not want to look at the fact that we deplete ourselves and are self-spent. We would rather just accept the "nice things" the preachers and teachers tell us. But that is not good enough. *You* have to be your own teacher and your own pupil. Who else can teach you freedom? When you are starving, your hunger is not appeased if someone else eats the meal.

The very questioning, "How would Socrates respond?" has in it the spaciousness that can bring us to that state "disembodied of materiality." If it was possible for Socrates, it is also possible for you and me. We do not need to live under illusions. It is possible to step out of it all. We can be free. Jesus confirmed this when he said,

> "...THE WORKS THAT I DO
> SHALL YE DO ALSO;
> AND GREATER WORKS THAN THESE
> SHALL YE DO..."[7]

Do you believe Jesus' words? Then know you too can come to freedom. It is possible. Each moment is perfect. Why postpone? Only the weak postpone and compromise. We can meet in this living moment and come to that state of freedom.

Why should you ever do anything in your life that cannot be experienced here and now? Do not believe in the past or the future. Here and now is the only truth and the only freedom. Are you willing to step out of the past? That is where fear is. And then it projects a future. If you have understood this you will also see how you project illusions. Fear is not a reality, but a projection. And all you have to do is to be free of your own projections. Honesty can dissolve them all. You will still make a living, so do not worry about losing your job. You might even get a better job, but this time you will be employed by God Himself. Isn't that nice?

How would Socrates respond? I have often wondered, if I were given the choice by Heaven to ask for a boon of anything I wanted, what would I ask for? Of all the choices, I would ask to be with an enlightened being. Just to observe how he lives — how he ties his shoelaces or closes the door, how he speaks. A person who extends the Will of God — what perfection it must be just to witness that! The company of the wise, of the virtuous, is a most precious thing.

What Socrates did was to neither deny nor accept what the oracle said. Instead, he set out to find the fact himself.

At that time there were rumors in Athens of a great scholar and philosopher, renowned for his wisdom. He had an enormous following. But upon hearing him, Socrates recognized that this man did not know the truth. He did not know reality; he was not related to the absolute. It was just a lot of talk, a lot of ideas. He was merely a preacher and that is why he had such a large following. Preachers do not challenge anyone and so they are successful. The minute the populace is challenged, they run for their lives because they do not really want freedom.

General gatherings were quite prevalent in Athens in those days. Socrates visited yet another meeting and another and he asked direct questions that must surely have been quite annoying to the promoters of ideas. Finally they got fed up with him and framed him, accusing him of corrupting the youth of Athens.

We are talking about a man who is free from fear and threatens our so-called civilization. Jesus did it too and you know what we did to Him.

Socrates, accused of corrupting the youth of Athens, stood before the court. After hearing the prosecuting lawyers he said to the jury, "I do not know what effect my accusers have had upon you, gentlemen, but for my own part I was almost carried away by them — their arguments were so convincing. On the other hand, scarcely a word of what they said was true."[8]

Watch out for vested interests. They are very persuasive. As long as we are not really interested in coming to consistency at all levels of our being, where duality ends, we will never know freedom. When we are interested in knowing about it and not the truth of it, the vested interests succeed.

Socrates was sentenced to be poisoned to death and was put in prison. Shortly before he was to drink the hemlock, one of his friends made arrangements for his escape. His friend urged Socrates to escape, saying that his death would hurt his family and friends, and would appear to the masses as weakness. But Socrates refused to adopt wrong means, and told his friend, "I cannot abandon the principles which I used to hold in the past simply because this accident has happened to me…"[9]

Socrates told his friends shortly before his death: "Evidently you think that I have less insight into the future than a swan; because when these birds feel that the time has come for them to die, they sing more loudly and sweetly than they have sung in all their lives before, for joy that they are going away into the presence of the god whose servants they are."[10]

A man who is independent is never afraid of consequences. He is part of the new, the unknown. Perhaps most of us *want* freedom but are frightened by the consequences. That is where the contradiction lies. Each person can be free from fear but we must first look into what it is that projects the consequences. We have to find out if consequences are real or not. Would you do that?

Since we project consequences, we can also dissolve those projections. We really can. In the very act of not projecting and pursuing, we will discover a strength within. It is instantaneous. Time does not come into it. We think everything takes time — but we must question that, too. Tell yourself, "I am not going to believe that either." Question everything. Begin to dissolve everything that your brain projects.

Everything in creation exists to help man to come to his perfection. You and I are not alone. Every single thing in creation assists us in discovering our own reality. And our reality is that we are created in the image of God. "God" is not a monopoly of any particular religion. "God" is not only Christian or Hindu or Moslem or Jewish. "God" existed before conventional religions ever came into being.

It is time that we demand freedom for ourselves. No one else can do it for us. It is not external; it is an internal action. We project consequences, "What will I do?" and so forth. But if we loved freedom, we would make inner correction. Once we are free, we will have the wisdom to do what we really want to do with our lives. Until then there is but conformity, and it makes life very dull, routine, and isolated; unrelated to anyone in a real way.

In freedom there is relationship, for there is love. There is no manipulation or dependence. And now I ask you, what objection do you have to being free? You have done a thousand things in your life. Has it ever gotten you to a moment of freedom? Neither your books nor your learning have helped. They are mere lullabies, keeping you asleep.

The discovery of your own reality, your own light, will not fit into anything. But, it will affect everything. Something happens upon the planet when one man comes to that state. He has nothing to preach for he is a light unto himself. So can you be.

> Why wait for Heaven? Those who seek the light are merely covering their eyes. The light is in them now. Enlightenment is but a recognition, not a change at all.... This light can not be lost. Why wait to find it in the future, or believe it has been lost already, or was never there?... The peace of God is shining in you now, and from your heart extends around the world. It pauses to caress each living thing, and leaves a blessing with it that remains forever and forever.[11]

Please do not underestimate yourself. It is not difficult; it is only a matter of decision. When you will not compromise, you will find you have strength and conviction, and nothing external can dominate you. Whatever you do, your heart will be in it, and it will be consistent at all levels of your being. What you do will be beautiful and essential. It will have the purity of innocence, uncontaminated by the past, for it is ever new.

You must trust in yourself to discover your own reality. You have the potential within to come to freedom — freedom from fear, freedom from self, freedom from illusion.

Know that you and God are not separate, nor are you separate from your brother. Knowing this, "Love ye one another" becomes your reality and all you can do is share your freedom.

CHAPTER FOUR

"Fear is not justified in any form."

Fear is deception. It attests that you have seen yourself as you could never be, and therefore look upon a world which is impossible. Not one thing in this world is true. It does not matter what the form in which it may appear. It witnesses but to your illusions of yourself. Let us not be deceived today. We are the Sons of God. There is no fear in us, for we are each a part of Love Itself.

A Course In Miracles
Workbook For Students
Lesson 240, page 402

4

LETTING GO
IS THE ISSUE —
DISCUSSIONS ON FEAR

WHAT SUBJECT SHOULD WE DISCUSS so that we can go beyond our knowing of ideas? Whatever subject we choose can begin to unfold and be a direct discovery of what it is in actuality. It can unfold its truth, its mystery, and its newness as we both give it the attention. What would you like to go into?

Student: Fear.

There are many kinds of fear. There is the fear of falling down if you are old, which is a physical fear. There is the fear of the dark. There is also the psychological fear that you will lose your job. There is a fear that someone might sue you or your money be stolen. Another fear may arise because you have a wife or husband you cannot trust.

You might call one fear insecurity. We see that fear can also be a suspicion or an anxiety about something we cannot control. If I feel that you can hurt me, then I want control and friction begins. We compete.

There are innumerable forms of fear. Knowing this, let's not leave fear as an abstract word. What particular kind of fear do you have?

> *Student:* I have numerous fears, but one that is very concrete to me is claustrophobia. I have such attacks that I have to leave my house and go out into open space. I panic. Claustrophobia is very real to me.

Why do you call it fear?

> *Student:* It seems like fear.

But why do you make it fear? Why not say, "I feel like being outdoors"?

> *Student:* When I have an attack, I have to alleviate the anxiety, the fear; and that's why I step out of the house or the room.

All right. Now let us see if we can give it another name. We could make you into a "naturalist" instead. [laughter] You see, once we have given something a label, we have to behave like it is so. We act it out. What's wrong with the bird that has been in a cage for a long time wanting to be out and fly? I don't think the bird is afraid.

It is important to know if there is something that interests you when you are not inside, under the roof. An awakened interest is a beautiful thing. You may very well be interested in nature or in looking at architecture, seeing shop windows, or observing people walking.

Just to be under the sky when it is filled with the light of the day vitalizes one with energies that are not of this earth. It connects us with our own wholeness, and opens us to the potentials of vision that are in us. Unknowingly, you may simply be drawn to what is natural.

The *Text* of *A Course In Miracles* states:

> *And therefore it is necessary that you have other experiences, more in line with truth, to teach you what is natural and true.*[1]

It is not natural for man to sit behind a desk most of the day. There are physiological and psychological consequences for confining oneself to an existence under the roof. The eyes are meant to see living things. How little we know about the vibration of colors and minerals that the eyes take in. When our seeing is direct, there is the peace of the sky filled with stars at night and the changing moods of light during the day.

So, what you call claustrophobia may be a wondrous thing to explore if we remove the bad connotation associated with the word.

Are we beginning to see the need to examine the sensation or emotion to which we give the power and complexity of a name? That is what we need to look at because we are here to dissolve fear. It does not matter which form it is in.

<u>We must see that thought is the basis of fear.</u> Is there fear without thought? Obviously we think with thought and we believe in what we think. Are not fear and thought synonymous? If you could see the truth of this, would you not be free of fear, irrespective of where you are?

Realizing the truth that there is no fear apart from thought allows us to transcend fear. But, for the most part, we just agree or disagree with this truth and remain at the thought level.

For instance, you could be walking in the woods and all of a sudden you discover you are lost. You may call it fear, but it is actually a sense of being lost, a sense of not having order. You do not know which way to go. That sensation is very natural and it demands that you come to the stillness of attention that has its own potential.

The feeling of being lost is not very pleasant, but it is natural. We do not need to call it fear.

One time I had gone to Florence, Italy. I was eager to see as much as I could because I was captivated by the beauty of the city. As soon as I put my luggage down in the hotel room, I rushed out and walked for five or more hours. I had a wonderful dinner and was thrilled with it all.

All of a sudden I realized I did not know how to get back. I did not even know the name of the hotel and so I couldn't ask anyone for directions. This gave me quite a jolt, but I did not call it fear. I had to make an immediate demand of my own resources to cope with the situation.

My need to find the way back to the hotel put me in contact with something that demanded attention, but that's not necessarily fear. Do you see that one would be confused for a moment, and then feel a sense of loss of control? This still may not be fear; it may just be lack of confidence in oneself.

And so, as I began to retrace my steps, I recognized different buildings by their architecture, recalled shop windows I had seen, and so on. I would stand at intersections and try to remember which street I had walked before, determined not to make a mistake. I walked for miles before I reached the hotel.

Do you see that it demanded a certain kind of responsibility and alertness on my part? Yet we tend to evade these challenges and call them fear.

Uncertainty is a most beautiful and natural state of man. Within it is the space for the unpredictable and the new which, in turn, add to the energy of awakening. To be in the bondage of the known and to feel secure in confinement is detrimental to one's life. In that state, we are lost in the assumption of our own littleness.

Much of what we think of as fear turns out to be something else. The next time you get afraid, ask yourself: "Am I really afraid, or is this just lack of confidence with which I defeat myself?" You will need space within to wonder about it. At least the fear will not be paralyzing you.

There is a different way of looking at a situation. Are we seeing that perhaps ninety percent of what we call fear is an unwillingness to question the authority of doubt and the limitation one imposes upon oneself? Wisdom lies in inner correction. Unless we demand honesty and precision of ourselves, there is no order in the mind.

Specificity is required in order to awaken a sense of awareness and discrimination. It stimulates a new faculty that makes your words responsible and forceful because you are fully aware and responsible for what you say. To awaken awareness and discrimination is our responsibility as human beings. It is in the recognition of truth that separation ends and one is in the moment that is not of time.

> *Student:* Last summer I was on the open sea and it was really rough. I was scared stiff. I thought we were going to sink, but it didn't happen. I think that was fear.

Can we agree that the function of the brain is to ensure survival, and that in this case survival is endangered? It's not a psychological fear. You're in the middle of a rough sea and it seems the boat will capsize. If you didn't get frightened I would have to ask, "What's the matter with you?"

There is something within the brain that seeks preservation and it is a very natural thing. Survival has its own intelligence. It does what it's supposed to do: it protects the physical body. So then, why do you call a natural thing "bad"? When I cut my finger, it hurts; and so I know to be more alert next time. If there was not the hurt to warn us, many of us would probably be missing fingers by now.

So, do you see that there is some intelligence to your feeling uneasy while in the middle of a rough sea?

May I share another story with you? One time I was swimming in Lake Como, in Italy. It was such a lovely evening with beautiful clouds overhead. I started to swim on my back, enthralled with the beauty of the sky. I swam on and on, totally forgetting about time or distance. By the time I realized I should turn around, I was about a mile and a half from shore.

Then I panicked and began to shout for help. There happened to be a lady who was also swimming in the lake at that time. I had noticed her on other days, swimming out quite far. At first I could sense her presence somewhere in the distance, but then I completely forgot about everything. And now I realized she was very far away. I tried to turn back towards shore but the water was already getting into my mouth.

I learned something even while drowning because I became so aware. I discovered that the voice carries much farther over water. And so the lady heard my shout. I saw her arm go up. And do you know, just the sight of her, just that human contact gave me so much strength!

But there was another thing I learned in that moment which was even more important. While in

India, I had met a very great being named Jayaprakash Narayan (for short, he was known as J.P.). When India attained her independence in 1947, Gandhi pronounced Jawaharlal Nehru and J.P. the two voices of India. Nehru, an exceptional statesman, was elected as the first Prime Minister of free India, and everyone wanted J.P. to take a high post in the Cabinet. The whole of India revered this selfless man who had given his life to humanism in this age of politics.

I was blessed to have a close relationship with him. Before I left India, he asked me, "Will you come back to India?" And I promised J.P. that I would be back.

Now, we come back to the scene in the middle of the lake where I was drowning. As I remembered my promise to J.P., I was energized by a strange courage that would not accept fear or helplessness. Can you imagine that? I said to myself, "I can't afford this nonsense of drowning. I have a promise to keep!" And I swam back to shore as if it was nothing.

What would you call that? Was it fear? What term would you use when you won't accept fear?

Why, then, do you want to conclude that fear is real? I would have died if I had. It is fear if I make it fear. But there is also something else within you, the will — that you promised the man! There is an indomitable will in each person that is stronger than fear and therefore, dispels it. Then you should ask: Is the will subject to fear? Each person can explore this much further.

Why is it that any little challenge becomes a threat? We have concluded so many things that hardly have any basis in fact. Whenever we are with the un-known, even for a moment, and the brain cannot respond adequately, we call it fear. I wonder who has ever directly experienced fear? I would like to meet that person.

> *Student:* It's exciting to hear this because if the fear pops up in me, I can ask myself, "What else can I do?"

If you have the time to say anything, it isn't fear. If you have the time to find an "alternative," then obviously it isn't fear; it is thought. We have probably never directly felt fear. We may know the intensity of self-consciousness that makes us freeze temporarily, but that is not fear.

I want to meet fear face-to-face where nothing intrudes upon it.

> *Student:* Is that possible?

I don't know, but in the meantime, I will not call anything else fear.

Fear has to be something we face directly. When it's direct, then you know it; until then, you cannot say if it is fear or not. We can't accept just any kind of phraseology about fear; we must look into the terms we use. Let us see if we can find fear. I'll be surprised if anyone even knows fear by the time we're through.

> *Student:* I had an experience that I think was fear. I was carrying my baby into the

> bathroom and when I was lowering her into the tub, a cobra raised its head and started hissing at me. I was fortunate to have been brought up in Africa, and so I knew to keep my eyes on the snake and not turn my back, that I must not make a sudden movement. Somehow I stepped backwards till I was out of the room, but I couldn't speak.

First, I don't have any objection to admitting fear. I'm not making a cause of proving there is no fear. But we can look at every new situation. Let's see what kind of attention we can give to that.

I don't think there is a person alive who would not freeze upon seeing a cobra — unless he's a snake charmer or a saint. As we have said, the survival instinct is natural and it has its own intelligence. Let's say it gives you a good warning when danger is at hand. You can call it a fear warning, but it has its own intelligence to cope with the emergency. Would you say, then, that physical fear has its own intelligence?

Student: Yes.

Here you are dealing with the actual cobra. It's not psychological. It's not the brain projecting another idea. The very fear itself, when you are in that kind of startling emergency situation, has its own potentials and intelligence. Why don't we admire that? There is the physical fear, but there is also the intelligence that knows what to do. The brain is afraid, but it can still function intelligently and rationally. Why not be grateful for this intelligence?

Physical fear is a natural response to danger. The fear we want to dispel is the psychological fear that we project when the thing hasn't even happened. Yet can we see that if it *does* happen, there is an intelligence that can cope with it? So then, why call it fear?

> *Student:* Why would a saint not be afraid of the cobra?

Possibly because he is startled and accepts it as a warning. He has reverence for life and honors the existence of the cobra. He would see that the eyes of the cobra perceive if he is threatened or not. The cobra is not a common reptile. He has faculties of which we know nothing. If you are panicky or hostile he would have to defend himself. And if you are calm then there is no danger, neither for you nor for the cobra.

Are we seeing this? When it is a sudden thing — whether you are on a rough sea, or you see a cobra, or you run into a rattlesnake — how you would act in that urgency would almost be independent of thought. It is something natural that is part of life and for which we have the skills and abilities to cope. We do have to venture out; we have to live in situations in which there are snakes and slippery ground and other dangers; but we can cope with them. If it were too safe, man would be rather dull.

Just look at the domesticated cow. Have you ever thought about how dull their reflexes are? I saw one of these cows in a field one time. I had a little car and I drove onto the field and headed right for it. I stopped about two feet away and it just stood there. About a minute later it finally got frightened and ran away. That kind of reflex would never survive in nature without the protection of barbed wire.

Have you seen how alert and quick the deer or gazelle is? If there were not the predators that eat them, they would have died out of laziness. The survival instinct keeps them alert. How nature has evolved different faculties to cope in life! That is part of evolution too. Doesn't it inspire you to observe this other intelligence? Why don't you look at life itself, just the wonder of it, how it does things? Just see how it works!

So what I am saying is that if, physically, you were never going to fall and you were never going to run into a snake or any other situation, you would probably be like that dumb cow. Would you prefer that? You'd hibernate more than ever and lead a really dull life. This domesticated life of routine is already dead enough. Perhaps that's why it keeps manufacturing violence.

> *Student:* Could we look at psychological fear? For instance, I'm afraid of the unknown.

Yes. We can go into that. There is a fear in us, that we can't relate with the eternal because we are afraid we would be nothing. That's a fear we need to deal with; it's a fear we can all identify with. Now, we want to see whether it is actually fear or not.

The fear of the unknown is a basic issue we need to deal with. Otherwise, the attachment to personality and its insecurity will rule our lives. Let us first see this fear as it is.

Fear is a concept of the relative thought system. In order to overcome fear, we need to understand the use of thought in making fear. How can we do this?

From the very outset, *A Course In Miracles* stresses the need to be exact and precise; it demands that we be factual and develop discrimination. In fact, the Course insists that we be very particular about each word we use.

For instance, Lesson 3 states:

> *The point of the exercises is to help you clear your mind of all past associations, to see things exactly as they appear to you now, and to realize how little you really understand about them. It is therefore essential that you keep a perfectly open mind, unhampered by judgment, in selecting the things to which the idea for the day is to be applied. For this purpose one thing is like another; equally suitable and therefore equally useful.*[2]

If we don't first see things as they are, we will project them as something else. Therefore, when we approach the absolute from the level of relative thought, there is fear because we are not seeing things as they are. We don't know what the absolute is; that is the unknown area. Shall we explore this?

First you will have to put your whole attention and interest into it. Otherwise, it will become an idea to you and you'll still be afraid. You must insist upon coming to the actuality and not settle for mere ideas. In some ways, we are like the domesticated cow; we have developed that kind of lazy mentality.

There are some things you and I have to do together; we have to share, to inquire, to explore. But we must make sure we don't get into learning because learning makes everything into an idea and therefore, no change takes place. Your fear remains intact.

The issue we want to deal with is the fear of the unknown. Let us see if it really is fear. And if it is, what can we do about it?

The Course tells us that fear is the opposite of love. We have read the Course, yet we still have fear. We can agree that the opposite of love is fear, but that is just an idea until we realize the truth of the statement.

The fact is, we don't know what love is; and fear is something we have projected. Yet we are here to see if it is possible to live without fear. If that is your intent, then you must question every idea in order to undo it and come to the actual state that is not afraid. If you don't put that kind of energy into it, you will remain pacified with ideas.

There is no question in my mind that it is possible to be free from fear — and not as an idea. But few people are willing to go all the way to the discovery of the truth.

We must "will" the mind not to be indiscriminate. Being exact and factual does not allow irrelevant thought to intrude. If you are truly attentive, irrelevant thought will not occur. When you give total attention, you will see the blessings of an energized mind that can undo deception and be clear in an instant. Miracles occur when you value inner correction, for the space the holy instant endows is timeless.

Lesson 42 states:

> *God is my Strength. Vision is His gift.*

> *You will see because it is the Will of God. It is His strength, not your own, that gives you power. And it is His gift, rather than your own, that offers vision to you.*

> *God is indeed your strength, and what He gives is truly given. This means that you can receive it any time and anywhere, wherever you are, and in whatever circumstance you find yourself.*[3]

Reading this should make you want to jump up and thank the heavens. You will also see it is all ordained; that your life is part of universal order.

So we see that ideas are something that we project. However, there is an attention that is so energetic it no longer projects. That attention has energy; or rather, attention *is* energy. Do you know that attention is impersonal? To know the truth of this is to be, for that moment, in a time-free state. When we are attentive, projection does not take place.

There is nothing anyone can do to make *you* attentive if you are not determined. If you can settle for an alternative, then you'll always have projected fear. And that is irresponsibility because when you accept fear, you live a dishonest life. As long as there is fear, your life is false. Can you make a commitment not to be dishonest to yourself?

The truth is there in the Course:

> *The opposite of love is fear, but what is all-encompassing can have no opposite.*[4]

> *Only perfect love exists.*
> *If there is fear,*
> *It produces a state that does not exist.*[5]

But what is the good of knowing this if you are still afraid? Knowing it as an idea does not solve the issue or dissolve the fear. Yet we are usually satisfied with verbal explanations. It is a rare person who would not settle for an idea. Are you committed that way?

Direct experience is the only thing that we must accept. And direct experience is only possible when you don't have an alternative to it, when you're not satisfied with stopping at the idea level. As the Course says:

> *My single purpose offers it to me.*[6]

As long as I think with the brain, which is physical, I am attached to my body, my personality. Fear,

personality, and being a body are all synonymous.
And as long as I continue to use the brain to try to
know the unknown, I am going to be afraid. Thought
cannot dissolve fear. If thought is not the means to
dissolving fear, then the next logical question would
be: what other means are there?

We see that the brain is physical and the brain
knows fear. However, the Course tells us there is
"love" and "forgiveness." These we do not know. Is
it possible to realize the absolute word? That is what
we want to explore.

> *Student:* That's the unknown?

Yes. We don't start with a conclusion that we know.
We start from the premise that we don't know.

> *Student:* I would like to say something about
> love. The feeling I had when I first saw
> my grandson was that of love. When I
> look for love or try to find out what
> love is, I always go back to that.

In everyone's life there are some of those moments.
But when those moments become memories they
become blocks, because you are again going back to
the brain. When people get all hung up about love, it
is usually a delusion. I am not here to deceive you.
Our purpose is to dissolve illusions, not add to them.
So, let's see what the illusions are.

Wisdom would not start from a conclusion because
a conclusion is something we project; it is something
with which we deceive ourselves. Can you see the

wisdom of this? This may be born out of love — freeing you from projecting conclusions and then seeking them! This, to me, is love and it's a miracle. Miracles cut time.

The way the human being has lived upon the planet is that he first projects an idea and then he pursues it. That's the way the human mind works: it projects and pursues. But that preoccupation has led us nowhere.

What kind of thought system would permit thinking without conclusions? Isn't our whole thought system one that seeks something?

But the thought system of God — of *A Course In Miracles* — is very different. And maybe that is the thought system that knows love. It is a thought system without conclusions.

What we *know* is the block. What we *know* is what limits us. When we can live a life without conclusions, where is the fear going to come from? If we don't have a conclusion, would we be afraid? Absolutely not.

Let's say, then, that fear and tomorrow are one and the same thing. Fear and time and personality have a relationship. And in that realm there are illusions. It is called *the sleep of forgetfulness,*[7] as the Course puts it. In *the sleep of forgetfulness* we project and we pursue, but we will never know truth. Love is totally absent.

It is important for us to discover that what we call "love" or "truth" are lies because our lives are false. Seeing this would bring us to humility. There is great intelligence in humility. It does not project big things; it just sees "what is." It sees: "This is what I am." In the seeing of that, who knows what would happen. It is not predictable because it would be something new. Instead of seeking and pursuing, it turns the tide.

> *Student:* If you don't have a goal, can you have a purpose?

I'm glad you asked that. The goal is the mischief, isn't it? The goal is something *you* project. When there is a goal, it is a source of conflict in your life. You are not at peace and you feel a sense of lack; you project a goal and then pursue fulfillment of the lack. And mankind dies never having stepped out of that trap.

Knowing this, you can be liberated. Knowing this, why would you project any goal? Wouldn't you give thanks that the source of conflict has been taken away?

Can you be grateful that now you see the way you have been living? Maybe there is love in this kind of wisdom. If the love were not there, do you think one could share this? The new is born out of gratefulness, not out of seeking goals. It is born out of your own gladness because something has touched you.

Would you take on the responsibility not to project a goal because that is what creates conflict? Can you bring that to application? When are you going to be true to yourself? Can you come to some conviction, some courage, and say, "I will never project a goal. This I will bring to application"? Isn't this enough to

93

transform you — that you will no longer create conflict in your life?

Love is a state in which there is no conflict. That is a law; it is true. The state of love is whole; therefore, conflict has ended. Have you received this gift? Are you going to stop projecting?

We have to see we are victims of projections and habits, and these are difficult to break away from. It takes courage to do so. The Course states:

It can be but myself I crucify.[8]

Why do we love our little self? Do we see that the little self always wants a big Self? I am here to take away the little self so that you can discover for your-self that you need not ever seek the other Self, for it is always with you.

> "The 'little I' seeks to enhance itself by external approval, external possessions and external 'love.' The Self that God created needs nothing. It is forever complete, safe, loved and loving. It seeks to share rather than to get; to extend rather than project."[9]

Can you picture a life that does not move from conclusions or projections, has no motives or pre-occupation? What would it be like?

Do you know the power of "I don't know," or the glory and the beauty of humility? There is space in you to bring all thoughts and knowing to an end. The one who comes to "I don't know" is certainly more at

peace. And from there, perhaps something else can begin.

When we say, "I know," it is a conclusion; and then we have to guard and protect our knowing. But when we say, "I don't know," the thoughts begin to have wider gaps between them. And in those gaps between the thoughts we can receive that which is not *of* thought. In the Course, He tells us:

> *If it helps you, think of me holding your hand and leading you. And I assure you this will be no idle fantasy.*[10]

What would you give for that? Who is ready to hold His hand? We are busy with our goals and our "knowings." How could we not be moved when we read:

> *I will teach with you and live with you if you will think with me...?*[11]

Do you want to think with Him? Then put away your conclusions. Don't project and pursue. See the mischief of having a goal and the conflict it creates. When you see the shortcoming of it, you'll put it aside. And to do so, you'll need a different way of thinking.

You'll discover that in projection, there is invariably the deception of self-improvement and the denial that you are already perfect and holy. Either you are perfect, or you are not. You can't have it both ways. If you are holy then that is what you will extend. Holiness extends holiness, not goals.

Either you are going to extend goals or you are going to end them. In order to think with Him, we have to put the goals away. But the brain always wants something to do; it wants a solution in which there is a doing. And it thinks it knows what that is. Whenever you think you know, you deceive yourself.

The thinking that we know is based on fear, self-centeredness, and attachment. But there is a thinking that is of a different quality. When He says, *...if you will think with me*, it means there are no consequences. Are we willing to find out what that kind of thinking is? We would have to let go of our own, would we not?

One of the characteristics of the human brain is that it hates uncertainty. We are all afraid of uncertainty, aren't we? We may have the resources to cope with the physical fear of being lost or of falling, but when we are faced with uncertainty, we don't know which way to turn.

Uncertainty wants certainty, and that's where we are caught. The fact is that we do not know what faith is.

...if you will think with me.

These are words rooted in faith; therefore, they do not have the fear of uncertainty in them. Faith is alive. It is a truth, not an idea. This is the thinking we need to be related to but have not yet known.

There is the danger of reading *...if you will think with me*, and making of this another goal. Please see the wisdom of this. The human brain that is afraid of uncertainty is also afraid of letting go. And unless we let go, we won't be able to think with Him. You may say, "Teach me how to think with Him." And I would say, "But you haven't let go of the conclusions and the projections yet." Unless we do, it won't work.

Several billion people have come and gone since He walked the earth — all of them trying to fulfill their own goals. We have plenty of energy for "wanting." There doesn't seem to be much for letting go.

How much falsehood there is in the world! Everything is for sale — Zen, meditation, mantras, even yoga. And because the appeal is to get more, not let go, it succeeds.

We live a life of choices, preferences, and advantages. Isn't that our present way of thinking? Where there are choices and advantages, there can be no decision to think with Him. That is why we are trying to point out: "See what the brain does. This is what limits it. It can't let go. It is afraid of uncertainty." To think with Him, letting go is essential.

All a brother can do is show you that what you thought was to your advantage is your bondage. And he tries to remove the blocks. That's all he can do.

But our preferences always favor remaining the way we are. We have the illusion of wanting to change, but we continue the same way internally. We keep on projecting, pursuing, and not letting go, constantly afraid of uncertainty.

It is time to wake up and come to another way of thinking — a thinking that is sane. The world needs sane people. You can no longer afford the luxury of your fear of uncertainty. You have a responsibility as a Son of God to bring something of the Kingdom to earth. And that Action of yours would be a light upon the earth — a strength to all mankind.

We must answer His call:

...if you will think with me.

And that means making the decision never to be afraid again, no matter what happens. Fear is an assumption in which we have placed our faith and trust. No one has to teach us trust; we already trust in our fears and insecurities! But our trust can be rightly used when we think with Him. And I can assure you, it is not all that difficult.

> *Student:* I am longing to ask you of your own experience with holding His hand. How do you put your hand in His?

When I have let go all other hands that I have projected. For there is only one hand — and that is His hand to you, to me.

> *Student:* Does that take courage?

It takes wisdom and intelligence. It comes with seeing the false as the false. Seeing the false has its own vitality to impart.

> *Student:* Having once done it, you would never want to live any other way?

98

No, it has no alternatives. If it did, it would be the same old preferences and conflict. It is what it is. I'm certain it is possible to come to; it is something we all can do. To the degree we do, the fear of the unknown will disappear and uncertainty will no longer be frightening.

> *How light and easy is the step across the narrow boundaries of the world of fear when you have recognized Whose hand you hold! Within your hand is everything you need to walk with perfect confidence away from fear forever, and to go straight on, and quickly reach the gate of Heaven itself.*[12]

Let us keep the words of the Holy Spirit in our hearts.

> *The truth is true. Nothing else matters, nothing else is real, and everything beside it is not there. Let Me make the one distinction for you that you cannot make, but need to learn. Your faith in nothing is deceiving you. Offer your faith to Me, and I will place it gently in the holy place where it belongs. You will find no deception there, but only the simple truth. And you will love it because you will understand it.*[13]

CHAPTER FIVE

The grace of God rests gently on forgiving eyes, and everything they look on speaks of Him to the beholder. He can see no evil; nothing in the world to fear, and no one who is different from himself. And as he loves them, so he looks upon himself with love and gentleness.

Salvation is no more than a reminder this world is not your home. Its laws are not imposed on you, its values are not yours. And this is seen and understood as each one takes his part in its undoing, as he did in making it.

A Course In Miracles
Text
pages 492-493

5

FEAR
IS NOT
A REALITY

LET US GO MORE DEEPLY into what fear is. We have seen that fear is not a reality. Although this statement should shock you, as we look at it together you will see the truth of it. Fear is not a reality; it is a conditioning.

From childhood we are conditioned to be afraid. It is not difficult to imagine the Navajos telling their children, "Watch out for those Hopis over there." If you are raised in France, your parents will tell you how bad the Germans are, and so on.

What values we teach our children! The biggest murderers in the world, who took away other people's freedom, are called "the Great." Napoleon the Great. Alexander the Great. I wonder if they would have called Genghis Khan "the Great"? If Germany had won the war, would Hitler have been called "the Great," too? The victor usually has the final word as far as history's interpretation goes.

So we see that psychological fear is born out of conditioning. We are conditioned to be afraid. And though we have made this conditioning real for us, it is not a reality. Conditioning always starts with an "if." We are told, "If you don't get good grades." Or, "If you don't do this or that…" "If" is not real, yet we have a forest of "ifs" in our brains. And with all the "ifs" and "buts," there is little spontaneity left.

The only reality is the living moment. Since we are not with the reality of the living moment, we project a tomorrow. Once we have projected a tomorrow, there is fear. Please see this because it is fundamental. Fear is always of tomorrow; you can never be afraid in the present. Fear is always of "a rainy day" sometime in the future. "What if somebody found out?" Or, "What if this or that happens?" But if you didn't project a tomorrow, you would never know fear and you would be capable of coping with anything.

Insurance is one of the largest businesses in the world today, and it is totally built on fear. What is insurance except the belief that we can protect ourselves from something we project might happen in the future? The temples of our civilization are the banks and insurance companies.

Fear is a projection and not a reality. Fear comes when you deny your own potential to love, and to be honest and just. Honesty is never afraid. Lack of conviction creates an organization of lawyers, police forces, and military powers to protect its own bondage, limitation, and unreality. When you are with reality, there are no projections because the grace of the present brings you to the inseparable wholeness of your being.

Our brains can project anything. We even project "God" with a big, long beard and a form that is bigger than we are. Why, if a horse could project a god, it, too, would be in his own image. He would have four strong legs and he would be the fastest runner and he would never allow anyone to sit!

> *Everything you recognize you identify with externals, something outside yourself. You cannot even think of God without a body, or in some form you think you recognize.... And while you limit your awareness to its tiny senses, you will not see the grandeur that surrounds you.*[1]

The brain can only project what it can see and it can't see anything that is not manifest. When we look at a flower, we seldom see the reality of the flower, the totality of it that is as large as the universe. We see the physical appearance but not the wholeness.

The Course describes the function of the body's eyes in this way:

> *See how the body's eyes rest on externals and cannot go beyond. Watch how they stop at nothingness, unable to go beyond the form to meaning. Nothing so blinding as perception of form. For sight of form means understanding has been obscured.*[2]

To see beyond the appearance, you would have to come to the clarity of your own being. And when you did, the flower would introduce you to the perfection that is already completed in nature in all its aspects.

As long as we can project a future, there will be some form of dread. There is no way we can avoid it. The Russians are afraid of the capitalists; the Americans are afraid of the Russians. All projections. You may say, "Well, if we don't project and we don't defend ourselves, they're going to kill us."

Is television teaching us to love peace rather than violence, war, and brutality? If violence were to spend a million dollars each day, it could not get better publicity than what is presently on television. When are we going to be responsible? When are we going to come to right values, to the discrimination that can say,

I will not value what is valueless ?[3]

Which one of us is going to say that and mean it? When you mean it and your words are true, you can no longer be affected by anything external. You won't ever fit into the falseness of any popular system. Being a man at peace with yourself, you will make no cause. You then have conviction and a voice of your own. And having the capacity to undo, you have already corrected reaction within yourself.

The wise never reacts, for his life is part of Action. It is this that gives him the space to be his own man, to be his own God-created Self. Maybe that is what Lincoln had.

Abraham Lincoln is the man who, all during the Civil War, never laughed because he was deeply concerned that thousands of human beings were being wounded and killed. Have we ever cared that deeply for anyone?

Lincoln did not laugh for three years out of concern for what was taking place. Have you ever seen a politician who isn't grinning most of the time? Today there are perhaps only two kinds of people who continually smile and laugh: the politicians and those who want to sell you something.

Lincoln was probably the greatest statesman America ever produced. His wisdom and his concern for human suffering are what kept the United States united. Lincoln knew the strength of rightness. He was humanistic; he was not a politician. Had he been a man of lesser quality and wisdom, this country would have been split. And once split, there would have been continual tension and rivalry between the two parts. Division always leads to friction. What do you think America would be today had it been divided? The Civil War would unquestionably have continued in different shapes and forms.

Please see the importance of this. We have areas of the world that are not at peace because they are divided. There is North Korea and South Korea, East and West Germany. Kashmir is divided between India and Pakistan. In a world run by vested interests and politics, there is always division.

When we are fragmented and distorted within, we fall into division and separation. And the unresolved areas of dispute are forever breeding hate. Then we look for a solution to settle the conflict. The Course describes our "solutions" thus:

> The world... sees a resolution as a state in which it is decided who shall win and who shall lose; how much the one shall take, and how much can the loser still defend. Yet does the problem still remain unsolved, for only justice can set up a state in which there is no loser; no one left unfairly treated and deprived, and thus with grounds for vengeance.[4]

Inevitably, it all leads to violence, which improves the military-industrial complex in one part of the world and brings bloodshed to another. Violence is a successful, cold-blooded commercial venture. And where a war economy thrives, the human being is put in the second place. It is a nightmare if you really see it.

Lincoln, the great and far-seeing humanist, had the wisdom to keep this nation united. One person. Listen to what he had to say:

> "At what point shall we expect the approach of danger? By what means shall we fortify against it? Shall we expect some trans-Atlantic military giant to step the ocean, and crush us at a blow?
>
> Never!
>
> All the armies of Europe, Asia and Africa combined... could not by force, take a drink

from the Ohio, or make a track on the Blue Ridge, in a trial of a thousand years.

Let us strive to deserve, as far as mortals may, the continued care of Divine Providence, trusting that, in future national emergencies, He will not fail to provide us the instruments of safety and security...

Let us have faith that right makes might."[5]

Lincoln is saying that if this nation stayed with rightness, it would be given the instruments of safety, and no nation of Europe, Asia, or Africa could ever invade it. Real strength lies in rightness — not weapons — for weapons are born out of the fear and weakness of man. When he resorts to violence, man is already defeated, for he violates the law of harmony, the Law of the Universe.

Lincoln, who knew the Eternal Law of the strength of rightness, left behind a wonderful formula for the rest of us to follow. His formula of "right makes might" is simple to follow, and you don't have to be president to do so.

We must change our values to honor Eternal Laws rather than manmade rules. When you abide by Eternal Laws, you are still respectful of manmade laws. You'll continue to drive on the right side of the street and you'll acknowledge when a policeman is doing his duty. That's respect. But your values go far beyond what is manmade.

A person who is wise and has his own ethics is an evolved human being, a civilized man. He will not take advantage of anyone. He lives a life of honesty and violates no laws.

Rightness has its own strength, and nothing that is of circumstances can snuff out the light it brings. It is the changeable that does not endure.

The strength of rightness is protected. It is that simple. Would you like to live by the strength of rightness and come to your own conviction? When you have your own integrity, you are fearless. We need to find that vitality, that conviction within.

Mere learning does not do it. Mere enthusiasm is still of the relative thought system and it does not mean a thing.

If we had the strength of rightness, would we be promoting violence? Billions of dollars are spent each year on military bases and warships. Eventually, it may well be this that defeats us and not a nuclear war.

Do you see what is happening in America today? Instead of using human energy to serve one another, we abuse it to sell. Our culture has fallen victim to commercialization, and must betray itself in the upsurge of selfish motives. The industrial economy we have created is leading this new nation astray, and will render it morally weak and spiritually helpless.

Lured by the glitter of success and wasteful indulgence, we have become a degenerate nation with a moral code based on money. We are buried in the interest of profit. The professionals have taken over the country; even the presidency is for sale. And the media, bought by money, comes out the winner. Even politics is subordinate to it.

We cannot correct society, but you and I can begin with ourselves. Simplicity is very beautiful. But to be simple you have to be wise. Wisdom does not pursue expedience and taking advantage. Where there are expedience and taking advantage, there is no relationship between man and man. In relationship, one is vulnerable. Only then can you say,

In my defenselessness my safety lies.[6]

That is relationship! Do you see how relationships are falling apart today, between wives and husbands as well as between parents and children? Everywhere there is more and more fragmentation and help-lessness. And we don't know what to do about it because in the absence of moral strength, we depend on the externals.

But the fact is, lack is never real. Only when we deny wholeness does lack seem real. It is this we need to see in order to be cleansed of fear and be sane. It is the sanity of the individual and the sanity of a nation that will bring peace to its people. When you come to a moment of wholeness, there is nothing external — there is only you. And when you are whole and related, you have something to give because what you give is of the Kingdom of God. You extend:

"THY KINGDOM COME.
THY WILL BE DONE IN EARTH,
AS IT IS IN HEAVEN."[7]

You give something that is not yours — and yet it is — and you are grateful you can share it with your brother. In the giving is the receiving. It is a richness you find within yourself. Now and then there were great beings who shared this wholeness and became examples for all of us. "In God We Trust" speaks of the perspective the Founding Fathers gave this nation.

Jesus, Whose holy teaching is to turn the cheek and love your enemy, instructs us:

"RESIST NOT EVIL."[8]

And now, in *A Course In Miracles*, He brings us to the peace of forgiveness. Jesus had outgrown reactions, resistance, and fear. These were the last and very powerful words He spoke:

"FATHER, FORGIVE THEM;
FOR THEY KNOW NOT WHAT THEY DO."[9]

Can you make it your business to discover the miracle of rightness? Would you live by that rightness even if you had to die for it? That would take conviction and integrity. That is not taught in our schools.

Freedom from fear is man's salvation. Truth makes irrelevant commercialized violence and the solutions of war. Where is there a man who would rather die than kill? His fearlessness is the sanity of humanity and the light of the world.

Can you say that you and rightness have become one? Have you learned that applying *A Course In Miracles* requires a rightness that is free from personal issues? That would take confidence and integrity.

Can we see that as long as there is personality, there is fear? Yet try to undo personality and you will discover how many defenses you have. We defend and justify our personalized existence. All we know is fear, with different names. Truth does not need any defense.

> *Defenses are the plans you undertake to make against the truth.... Let no defenses but your present trust direct the future, and this life becomes a meaningful encounter with the truth that only your defenses would conceal.*[10]

There is no way you can avoid the challenge this presents unless you settle for a conclusion. You will probably go just so far, and then conclude: "I'm helpless. I don't think I can undo my personality and fear." The fact is, you can do it.

The vitality of objective thought, the flower of wisdom, can undo your conclusions. We need to question and undo our opinion about the world we live in. We must find the resources within ourselves to face the fear; we must accept the challenge of going beyond conclusions and "knowings."

It is possible to live a life free of consequences, a life that has no fear in it. But it is not possible without coming to the meaning of "know thyself" which brings you to a sense of responsibility and self-honesty.

Yet "know thyself" has become almost impossible to realize. And love and truth have become remote and unnecessary in a world obsessed with the physical.

Why has mankind turned to the ways of cruelty, aggression, fear, and sorrow? Why has he not turned within to realize his own wholeness and the glory of his God-given perfection? Why has a substitute, an alternative become so important in this industrial age of educated ignorance? Why did man choose the physical body of illusions instead of the purity of eternal spirit that he is? Why do we settle for the limitation of fear and personality rather than knowing the actual state of rightness? Don't you want to find out what prevents the application of rightness in your own life? Can you receive the gift of rightness now? If you can't, then why go on reading books?

Without application, truth remains an empty word. Ideas have no meaning; they are a waste of life. Analyzing things intellectually and being satisfied with ideas is not application. Love and rightness remain unknown to the relative thought system by which we are educated to live. You may have the illusion of "helping people," but so-called "helping others" is a pretense. Without love and rightness, there is no such thing as being "helpful."

When you realize what rightness is, the Action of Heaven takes place within you. You have no need to plan, scheme and project. Having discovered it in yourself, you lead your brothers and sisters to the perfection that God has created in them.

Every single one of us is capable of bringing rightness to application in our life. Why then do we stay with half-measures? What prevents you from taking the step to an Action that is of Life? Why is your life not an expression of rightness?

There is wisdom in self-knowledge. If we inquire, the Holy Spirit is there to help us undo misperceptions. But we are not in need of the Holy Spirit because we are not deeply interested in self-transformation. For the most part, we value learning but not the wisdom of undoing our pretenses and deceptions.

We have to start somewhere to make the changes within, and rightness begins at a very simple level. There is wisdom in simplicity and in doing without the unessential. To be constantly lonely, bored, and preoccupied with desires is to degrade yourself. Why don't we have the conviction to say "no" to distractions, and "yes" to meeting another's need?

In rightness there is no conflict because rightness is not of thought. The verbal does not touch it. In rightness, you are whole. And your life is a blessing upon the earth. Then you can say,

> "THY WILL BE DONE IN EARTH,
> AS IT IS IN HEAVEN."

Then you will find that you can forgive all things because you are with newness; the past does not intrude on you. And whatever you do will have meaning, whether you cook vegetables or wash clothes. You will be totally present, in right relationship with all that is.

To be present is to come to a vitality and a joy you have never known before. And the peace within you that knows no fear is what you share with another. You recognize what is meaningless and therefore your life becomes simplified. You need less, but you have a lot more to give.

One who is present does not get taken over by other people's problems or projects that are born out of self-centeredness. All problems seem insignificant in a moment of silence. Problems disappear like darkness disappears before the light. And you are the light. You assure others that rightness is within them, too, for God has created them perfect, along with you.

Lesson 156 of the Course states:

> *There is a light in you which cannot die; whose presence is so holy that the world is sanctified because of you. All things that live bring gifts to you, and offer them in gratitude and gladness at your feet. The scent of flowers is their gift to you. The waves bow down before you, and the trees extend their arms to shield you from the heat, and lay their leaves before you on the ground that you may walk in softness, while the wind sinks to a whisper round your holy head....*

This is the way salvation works. As you step back, the light in you steps forward and encompasses the world.[11]

Do you see that rightness is a state of being in which you have something to give, in place of the sense of lack that we impose upon ourselves? With rightness you have no need of vanity, insecurity, or boredom. You care. And you become creative. Whatever you do is essential. You respond to a need rather than to wishes and wantings. And the laughter within you is a dance upon the earth, a song of joy. Would you not feel free knowing that all your needs are met?

He will go before you making straight your path, and leaving in your way no stones to trip on, and no obstacles to bar your way. Nothing you need will be denied you. Not one seeming difficulty but will melt away before you reach it. You need take thought for nothing, careless of everything except the only purpose that you would fulfill. As that was given you, so will its fulfillment be. God's guarantee will hold against all obstacles, for it rests on certainty and not contingency. It rests on you. And what can be more certain than a Son of God?[12]

In rightness, ambition does not intrude upon you. You are free. You touch people but not with wantings or with projects, with ambition or success. These are of mortal values and have no meaning. You touch them with your love.

If there is no love in our hearts, then what else can we expect but violence and war, inflation and cancer, drugs and adultery? It is one big Babylon. We are not at peace with ourselves.

To be at peace is to be present. And when you are present, you hold hands with God. You have the space to listen to His words. The still small voice is ever with you.

> *How instantly the memory of God arises in the mind that has no fear to keep the memory away! Its own remembering has gone. There is no past to keep its fearful image in the way of glad awakening to present peace.*[13]

To be at peace is to want nothing. In this accelerated and highly stimulated era, we are always wanting things to be other than the way they are. The wise never contaminates his mind with a wish for things of the earth; therefore, he is at peace. Hear the words of a true poet.

> "The heart of a king trembles
> before a man who wants nothing."
>
> Mohammed Iqubal[14]

That is the voice of peace and of love. It has discovered the Source is God.

The fact is, the peace of God is in the eternal present. There is never a moment when His grace is not flowing. But we choose to put our faith in dogmas and political and economic systems. They do not work. Only love works; only the grace of God works.

When you are at peace within and free from fear, you no longer fit into systems. You are as vast as creation itself. You are not regulated by brain activity, for you are part of the Mind of God — never separate from Him or from your brother.

Plans and projects and dogmas have no reality whatsoever. They are fool's gold, full of deceptions. If you cannot receive the grace of God and you cannot discover your own peace, what makes you think that external institutions are going to do it for you? If you don't love yourself, how can you love another?

To be at peace is to know your own glory, as God created you. Yet when we get caught in manmade ideas, there is a "you" and a "me," and friction results. We are in conflict within and we think that is quite normal. We even accept fear as being normal.

You have a challenge before you because only rightness and love are religious. How do you come to rightness? By discovering that you are always deviating from it. This activity of evasion is promoted by thought, and that is of your own making. There is nothing to achieve; you merely have to see the deception of your own projections. There is rightness in seeing the deception; in pursuing the deception, there are consequences.

Life is a great responsibility. No one can force you to take the step. But *A Course In Miracles* has come to lead the way. Read the Course with all your heart and mind, and be receptive to the True Knowledge it imparts. Give each lesson the purity of your attention, and be intent on bringing it to application.

Challenge yourself to transcend your body senses. By bringing learning to an end, you will recognize the potential of your own stillness.

How is rightness realized? Do not accept fear as real, and rightness will have its own Action.

CHAPTER SIX

The concept of the self has always been the great preoccupation of the world. And everyone believes that he must find the answer to the riddle of himself.... There will come a time when images have all gone by, and you will see you know not what you are. It is to this unsealed and open mind that truth returns, unhindered and unbound. Where concepts of the self have been laid by is truth revealed exactly as it is.

A Course In Miracles
Text
page 613

6
INDIVIDUALITY

ALL THROUGH THE AGES man has placed a great deal of emphasis on asserting his individuality. This isolation into individuality has been a curse, and we have adored it all along. Individuality can also be called "personality" or "ego" or "self-centeredness."

A wise person starts with the reversal of this process — he starts with what may be called "undoing." Jesus came and turned over the money-changers' tables. Moses came and challenged the Pharaoh's system. No wise person has come who did not start with undoing. The clergy confirms beliefs while prophets and saints undo them. They reverse the process. Our belief systems and dogmas are as bad as the individuality in which we are imprisoned.

Why not become aware of the traits of individuality? See how false and limiting individuality really is. Each person can discover what a lie he lives. Get to know yourself and perhaps you won't boast so much about "individuality." Maybe then the voice of undoing will be heeded.

What, in essence, is individuality? Mr. Krishnamurti has said, "The word 'individual' means one who is not divisible, who is whole — not fragmented." Yet to the world the individual is a separate entity and, as we have seen, individuality is actually equated with fear. It has many other names also: insecurity, unfulfillment, survival, a sense of lack, whatever. But it still remains fear. Can you imagine dying never having outgrown the illusion of separation from wholeness? Man is more in the grip of fear today than at any other time in the history of the world. We do not even have our own work; now we have to get a job and be a mercenary.

Even our children are not free. They are drafted into school at an early age to be trained to fit into a career. And who the child is, with all his inner potentials remaining dormant, is generally ignored. Why? Because we are insecure and we feel we have to survive. There is violence in survival and ambition. But there is a peace within the child and an impeccable place within you that is holy and knows the True Knowledge of One Reality that is.

As long as there is fear, the body sensations will never let you know there is something else beyond time and individuality. Live with it. Find out how it works. Get to know yourself. Any single thing you say is not true; it is usually an opinion, an assumption that is neither intelligent nor your own. The collective mind is heavily conditioned and most people have

never uttered a single truth in their lives, separated
as they are from their own timelessness.

What is preventing you from salvation? A false
sense of separate identity, is it not? Individuality is a
misuse of energy and time. Have you ever questioned
it? If you did, you would be an extension of the Will
of God, which in truth is your will also. You would
have the vitality to remove all doubts — which is
harder than moving mountains.

Either there is fear — individuality — or there is
gratefulness. When you are grateful, you see and hear
directly. Nothing deceives you, nothing passes by
unnoticed. You have an awareness that is bigger than
individuality. Without awareness, you are merely
dozing, asleep in a delirium of illusions and you
cannot heed anything.

You can agree with all this, but are you merely
being influenced? It makes no difference whether
people agree or disagree. But those who, by just
listening, come to gratefulness can step out of this
bondage.

Only when we free ourselves from fear can we
experience gratefulness directly. Our whole thought
system changes and we are related to God's Plan for
Salvation, not with the projected plans of the ego.

And what is God's Plan for Salvation? God's Plan
is to free us from illusions and unreality. But we never
use gratefulness and awareness to dissolve unreality.
And unreality, whether in this or in another country,

whether in this or in any other century, is always of fear and requires costly armies to maintain itself.

A Course In Miracles comes along and is given directly to you, to me. What if you were really to know what the Course is? Would you not be grateful? Would there not be the happiness? One way you can tell if it is real to you is to see if you are grateful and at peace. You are getting away from influence then, are you not? Away from the influence of your own thoughts as well as another's. Then something has been undone. Some light has come into you. And it is possible this day to have that clarity — the light that eliminates all fear.

Fear is an effect of ignorance, and both can be dissolved by the light of gratefulness. Gratefulness imparts an energy so vast it is beyond individuality. Its resources are unlimited. Its action is an *Action.* Anything individuality will ever do, no matter how good it may seem according to the world's standards, is still going to be *reaction* because it is subject to the laws of cause and effect.

Individuality is part of reaction, not Action, because it is regulated by things of time. It does not extend anything from Heaven or from the light within. It merely changes things at the time level. Which would you rather do with your energy: change things at the relative level or receive this inner light which is Action itself?

As long as we limit ourselves to individuality we are not bringing the Kingdom of God to earth. *A Course In Miracles* tells us:

No one can fail who seeks to reach the truth.[1]

And no one will succeed who limits his interests to things of time no matter how much he has worked, or how much "good" he has done, because it is still part of reaction.

Reaction is an energy that dissipates. It is not related to the Source and therefore, does not have Its resources. Only Action has. It is called the creative Action of Life and is outside the realm of time.

Can we, then, value salvation? Can we make the change from fear to gratefulness, to something that is beyond individuality? Gratefulness is an awareness of that which is beyond individuality. It brings with it a new wisdom, a new joy. It must start with giving because it *has* something to give. It is so simple. What it gives is eternal and therefore it is inexhaustible. It dissolves all notions of littleness.

Having something to give is the key to happiness. What you have to give to your brother may be called love or truth or strength but it is not yours; it becomes yours own only when you give it. That is the secret of holy relationship and the wisdom that the Holy Spirit imparts. Your brother is not separate from you and there is no individuality separating you from him.

There is only One Life — so holy, so sacred. It is something the senses would never know, but in that Presence even the senses become totally still. You discover you are not a body but the Un-nameable.

Can we truly see that individuality and fear are one and the same thing? Then we have a function before us. The function is to observe how we maintain our individuality, how we make sure it never touches upon gratefulness because gratefulness is not of physical sensations. It is something within, independent of the body and its senses.

The minute you have individuality, you are connected with the externals because *you* are then external to your own reality. If you are external, you will be affected by the externals. But gratefulness is independent of the externals. It remains forever unaffected.

The truth is that there is peace and joy in life and we must find this peace within. It must be your own direct experience. Unless you feel the gratefulness and peace within, you have understood nothing. Mere understanding is of misunderstanding; it is an illusion. Insist on knowing peace and gratefulness directly because as long as you do not know them, you will be influenced and remain regulated by the physical senses and their preoccupation with nothingness.

Insist upon direct knowing. Let that be your decision. Unless you and I have come to gratefulness and peace, the future will be our master and we will live by the fear of consequences. Take a stand not to be regulated by your "knowings" and the future will have less sway over you. The commitment not to let your assumptions or ideas influence you brings with it its own awareness.

Can we do it now, this moment? The discovery begins simply. You can say: "I have discovered there are some things I can cope with and so the future does not scare me. But with other things the future is still there and it frightens me. I am glad I am becoming more aware of it." It is like Jacob wrestling with the Angel — the "angel" being the future.[2] You will be far more attentive when you begin making your own discoveries.

It is possible for us to dissolve the notions of the future to a certain degree and to feel good about that, but on other issues we may not be able to do so as readily because they could still take us over. At least you are beginning to see the difficulties involved — that in spite of your good intentions, certain things can still get the better of you. No one is going to condemn you for it.

As long as you are with peace and gratefulness you will have a much stronger base from which to work. You will have created some space within you — and that space *is* gratefulness. The minute you have been touched by gratefulness, the illusions will begin to dissolve. That action is like a new birth: once the child is born, he continues to grow effortlessly.

Gratefulness relates us to all of creation because it is not of the body senses. What a nice way to step out of individuality — and a happy one. You do not need to sit on a board of nails. How could something of God be sorrowful?

Gratefulness is a gift of Heaven because it is independent of individuality. Peace is a gift of God because it is not of the earth. Once you have received it, you extend it effortlessly. There is no thought in it. It does not project and then pursue. When peace and gratefulness are not there, we extend fear and insecurity.

Peace extends peace. Fear extends fear. Whatever a thing is, it has the knowledge of its own existence and that is what it extends. An orange seed grows an orange tree. A gopher is a gopher and will remain a gopher. Each continues to extend what it is. Man began with a tribal approach and today we have nationalism — glorified tribalism. Tribalism began with fear and fear is no less today. Yet man's reality is not fear; it is peace. And this is what we need to discover and extend.

When peace is your direct experience, your gratefulness then extends it. But in order to come to that kind of extension, you have to undo individuality. Until you are grateful, you are still at the horizontal plane. Until you are at peace, you are still with thought and relative knowledge.

There is an urgency to end the deception of thought and come to clarity. Clarity is freedom from thought; therefore, freedom from fear. In clarity, the dread of the future is over because you recognize *you* are the one who projected it. In the present there is no such thing as fear. This is some statement! In the present there is no such thing as fear because if you can be in the present, you will not interfere. Why? Because you see the perfection of what is and you are grateful and at peace. How could fear be real then?

Having understood this, you won't give such importance to future projections. Knowing this, are you at peace? Are you grateful? Are you clear? Unless this becomes your own experience, all the rest is make-believe and part of unreality.

When you can say, *Nothing real can be threatened,* you are in the present and therefore, out of time — past and future.

Will you now make this part of your memory so that you will know its strength whenever you are tempted to project some fear or consequences?

Nothing unreal exists.

See that it is not real. Tell yourself in your own voice, "I no longer live by unreality." When are you going to hear your own voice? It is within you.

When a person utters a truth, the light of that truth never leaves this plane because it is part of eternity. How can it leave? But it changes the vibrations of the planet. Prophets of God and saints and sages have come and uttered words that uplifted the vibration of the planet because their words were true. Centuries pass by, but the energy of their words never diminishes. It remains for all time.

Do you not want to have a voice of your own — a voice that is true; a voice that is not of individuality; a voice that makes the Kingdom of God alive upon the earth? Make the decision:

My single purpose offers it to me.[3]

And you will have all the strength you need. When you have the strength of *single purpose* you have something greater than individuality. You will never compromise out of helplessness and the future will no longer frighten you. The decision is yours.

CHAPTER SEVEN

"I am affected only by my thoughts."

It needs but this to let salvation come to all the world. For in this single thought is everyone released at last from fear. Now has he learned that no one frightens him, and nothing can endanger him. He has no enemies, and he is safe from all external things. His thoughts can frighten him, but since these thoughts belong to him alone, he has the power to change them and exchange each fear thought for a happy thought of love....

"Your plan is sure, my Father, — only Yours. All other plans will fail. And I will have thoughts that will frighten me, until I learn that You have given me the only Thought that leads me to salvation. Mine alone will fail, and lead me nowhere. But the Thought You gave me promises to lead me home, because it holds your promise to Your Son."

A Course In Miracles
Workbook For Students
Lesson 338, page 461

7

ULTIMATELY
WE HAVE TO
CONQUER FEAR

THE PURITY OF SILENCE makes all things one. In silence, you hear the song of birds in the distance and the distance disappears. The birds sing within you and you hear the song of everything in creation singing the praise of God. The joy of its own perfection praises the Creator.

Have you ever observed your own perfection and given thanks? Then your life, too, would be a song. Every breath would convey your adoration. To see perfection in yourself and in a brother becomes the function of each one, until there is no imperfection or misperception, and you realize that, beyond appearances, there is no "other," only God.

In that state one can say with certainty:

I place the future in the Hands of God.[1]

What does this mean? It means you have come to a state of stillness in which there is no past or future. Stillness is an egoless state that lives in trust and faith.

Trust and faith have tremendous power. Their power is a current that takes you through all experience, untouched by anything of the earth. As you leave duality behind, you realize there is an Action within stillness that is creative. The Will of God becomes a movement through you and you let It express Itself while you remain an extension of wholeness.

Each one of us has the potential to come to the state that can say:

I place the future in the Hands of God.

If this is what we are determined to do, it is not difficult. Only the habits that keep us preoccupied stand in the way of determination. We need not justify our irresponsibility. What prevents us from coming to seriousness? That state is within reach. Can we say we do not want it?

Without stillness, with its purity of silence and trust, there are the impurities within that activate desires and projections. Desires, urges, and impulses come into being out of a sense of lack and prevent us from knowing that we are God-like. Yet the world of the senses is unreal. And what is real in us is what undoes illusion. The Course states:

I do not perceive my own best interests.[2]

But the fact is:

> *I am sustained by the Love of God.*[3]

The Course also says:

> *Spirit am I, a holy Son of God.*
> *Free of all limits, safe and healed and whole,*
> *Free to forgive, and free to save the world.*[4]

We need to discover that in stillness lies the power that rules the universe. In stillness we can do anything, because that stillness acts through us in whatever we do. That is what is meant by Action in which we extend what we are. Extension means there is no separation. Are we not to extend stillness, non-motivation, and trust in God?

If we act from any other reason, it is of relative knowledge and therefore, of personality. Why is it so difficult for us to let go of relative knowledge? Although we rationally understand that we need to let go, it is still very difficult.

We must find out what those forces* are that refuse to let go of relative knowledge. Are they self-generated? Are they actual or are they things that our attachment gives reality to? There are forces in the world that are very efficient: they creep in, take over, and constantly make us feel helpless. Don't you feel helpless when challenged?

---

* For further discussion of the forces of illusion, see "Dark Forces" in *The Future Of Mankind — The Branching Of The Road* by Tara Singh (Foundation For Life Action, 1986), pages 59-68. (Editor)

What are these forces? They are called "illusions." Illusions are based on unfulfillment and therefore, are always seeking, always busy with "becoming" and "self-improvement."

Can we start to discover how great a part the illusion of "becoming" plays in our lives, how it cripples us? How did it come into being? We see the plants and animals on this planet are just as subject to competition and to struggle as we are. But what is different about man? One difference is that plants and animals do not project illusions. A plant never wants to be something other than what it is. Are not all of the projections man lives by illusions? They are part of the earth forces, or earth energies.*

Earth energy is natural. It grows trees and fruits. Its extension is a continuation of what it is. The earth provides us with everything we need to survive. But illusions are manmade. They are of our own making and keep us bound to the energy of the earth.

Do we see that our relative thought system promotes unreality? Seeing this, what is the appropriate response? We have to take action because a fact has been brought to attention. What we do with it is our responsibility. We can be grateful that this has been made clear — that we are caught in the deception of self-projected images which beguile us, and that is the world in which we live. But something else exists beyond illusions that is not part of

---

* For detailed exploration into "earth energies," see "Why Has There Always Been War In The World?" in *The Future Of Mankind — The Branching Of The Road* by Tara Singh, pages 25-40. (Editor)

deception. We do not yet know what that is, and we need to discover it.

Why is it we avoid meeting this crisis? Why are we complacent? We are caught in illusion; we are deceived by illusion. Illusion and thought are one and the same thing. Now, what are we going to do about it? That is the question, isn't it? What would we answer? Take a moment to ponder over this.

And now we must ask, in answering this question, are you not still acting through thought? Is that not an illusion, too?

The minute thought is questioned we feel helpless, don't we? And when someone questions our thought system, we feel attacked. Please see this. Could it be any simpler? It is presented without complication, without philosophy, just as a fact we can see.

Is it possible to put an end to illusion? If we *do* anything, it is again motivated and activated by thought. Whatever we propose to do is again of thought. Can we discover how dependent we are on thought? This is some discovery! We are so dependent on thought that we try to solve every problem with it. And we really believe we can, although we never have.

How blessed we are to have *A Course In Miracles* to bring us to crisis. We have been too comfortable in our illusions. We live and die in our illusions because we go to thought — which is also an illusion — to solve the issue. Can we keep the fire of discontent burning within us? If we do not, we will eventually give up and say we cannot dissolve our illusions.

Unless we have reverence for the Course and the truth it imparts, we will not be able to receive what it has to give. There are many pitfalls along the way. We will inevitably jump to this conclusion or that assumption and never come to the intensity of attention and reverence where truth can be received. Without reverence we deny ourselves the possibility of ever receiving. Are we beginning to see how important reverence is?

There are teachers who have promised all kinds of things, but when have we known a teacher who says, *"You* are perfect. The rest is all illusion"? And he makes the demand of you that *you* discover it. That is the role of an ordained teacher of *A Course In Miracles.* He demands that you come to your own freedom because you are your own light. Therefore, he does not *teach* you anything but it becomes a joint discovery where both can learn. Isn't that beautiful? Those who are interested in giving or accumulating knowledge are merely collecting phraseology. They become detrimental to themselves because they deny themselves the possibility of ever knowing truth.

If we loved truth we would come to crisis. Somehow we are too comfortable. At one time or another we have probably all thought: "If I could just know what to do. I want clarity. I want to know God and truth." In our search for answers we have travelled thousands of miles — but what about this one movement of an inch? It is such a small step. Why are we now putting roadblocks before it? We have waited so long for clarity, what objections do we have to coming to it now, this instant? We cannot say that in this moment that possibility does not exist. What prevents that action now? Each person must find out.

We have seen that thought is illusion. Why don't we open up and expose the illusion? Everyone has thoughts, and therefore, illusions; and we need to dissolve them. It requires our cooperation. We must empty ourselves of our conclusions, our "knowings," and our assumptions, so that we can directly discover that thought has no validity. Why don't we want to make that direct discovery? We can all say, "All right, I have thoughts and I am caught in the illusion of thought." But why don't we want to be free of it?

First, thought keeps us preoccupied. Then, when we shepherd thought into one place and put a spotlight on it, it goes into hibernation. See the cleverness of thought that does not want to expose itself. Thought is afraid to be dissolved, and that is the illusion. It can pretend it knows or it doesn't know. It is so elusive.

We have to confront our thoughts. If not now, later. But when it finally happens, the issue will always be confronted in the present. How long do we want to drag on and live at the level of time?

Time exists only in the world of illusion, the world of thought. Thought invents time in order to postpone. It is never going to face itself. It will say, "Wait a minute. If I hadn't had such a big meal, or if I wasn't sleepy," and so on.

Thought *is* unfulfillment. Therefore, it constantly capitalizes on unfulfillment. It is always going to delay and think it needs some other circumstances or situation. "If only this wasn't so, I could do it." Thought will never see its own deceptions. Can you imagine that thought invented time in order to postpone the present? And when we are not in the present, we dissipate our energy. It is a waste of life.

The present has enormous vitality; it has the power of creation in it. But thought prevents us from entering into the present. Why? Because thought is part of earth energies, the forces of illusion. The impact of earth energies is strong in all of us. Are we beginning to see that illusions are also self-destructive? We do not have to worry about dinosaurs out there, they are inside each of us. Every person must deal with the illusions of thought. That is the task ahead of us. That is the challenge facing man who is caught in time and wants to step into his real nature, into eternity. Pray that we can keep this challenge alive in us.

If we keep the challenge alive, we will come to a state of discontent — that we simply cannot and will not live in illusion. When we discover that determination, the illusions are going to show us some frightful sights: no one is going to take care of us; we are going to die, and so forth.

To extend the Will of God is our true function. But right now we are extending fear and the illusion of thought. And the world is in chaos. We are part of that chaos because we are part of the illusion of thought that made it. Ultimately we have to conquer fear, for fear is the biggest illusion. To overcome fear we will need conviction.

A man who brings illusions to truth is inspired by gratefulness — gratefulness to life for giving him that opportunity. He need never feel defeated. However, thought can never be grateful. It knows to say "thank you" when it receives something, but gratefulness is much more than that. Gratefulness is born out of inspiration, not thought.

Thought is never going to do anything holy. It can read the scriptures — but even that is a preoccupation to busy itself. Boredom does not care if it is pain or pleasure; it just wants activity. Would you believe that? Our thought has its own "non-intelligence," so to speak, and we are ruled by it.

Part of the activity of thought is the preoccupation with "becoming." Our thought system, which is based on illusion, believes in "becoming." That is why the word "how" came into our vocabulary. "How do I become this? How do I do that?" The illusion of thought is that, because it is unfulfilled, it always wants to "become." The fact is, as long as we are with thought, we will remain unfulfilled.

"Becoming" is an activity of thought and thought keeps illusion alive. Is this clear? As long as I am part of thought, I am unfulfilled and preoccupied with "becoming." And how do I "become"? I project and then I pursue. I want to be religious. I want to be rich. I want to go to Yosemite. These are all projections.

My thoughts are images that I have made.[5]

Are we coming to know the truth of this now?

Although it has three hundred and sixty-five lessons, *A Course In Miracles* does not advocate "becoming." It does not promote postponement because each day it imparts a truth that has the potential to free you immediately. Each lesson carries its own benediction, its own vibration to bring you to the truth. This is clearly stated in Lesson 109.

I rest in God.

This thought has power
to wake the sleeping truth in you...[6]

Yet we are caught in the activity of "becoming." Seeing this, the natural question would then be: "What else is there?" There is a state of BEING in which one is free from illusions, from thought, and from belief in "me and mine." To BE is to be free from time, from the "how" of "becoming," and from the activity of illusion. And yet it is so difficult for us to let go of the illusion of thought. Perhaps there is nothing else to learn.

God's Thought — which is our real thought, not that of brain activity — is always within us but we do not heed it. *A Course In Miracles* is an expression of God's Thought trying to reach us through external means. Can we see the compassion of God, that if we do not hear His Thought in one lesson, maybe we will hear it in another?

To come to the Thoughts of God requires consistency at all levels of our being. That means being intensely energetic — so energetic that our thought cannot intrude. Thought only intrudes when we are preoccupied with different levels — usually lower levels — that are never whole. For the most part, we live a partial existence, quite content with a meaningless life.

In order to see deception, we have to be smarter than thought. That means not using thought. There is a *seeing* that is not of thought. This is called *awareness*. Awareness creates an intensity within us when we realize the mess we are in and no longer want to stay in it. But as long as we are content with being deceived, we will be incapable of coming to intensity. We will say, "Tomorrow I'm going to do it."

When we no longer get so completely taken over by thought, there is a remembrance of something more. As we step out of the tremendous pressure of thought that consumes us, we are no longer ruled by thought and miracles abound. Just one moment of innocence — some gap between the thoughts — and a miracle takes place.

That space between the thoughts is a call for help — though it is not necessarily calling with thought. The desire to turn to the internal, to the quiet in you rather than to the understanding of thought, is a blessing that is given. HE is already leading you by the hand, otherwise you could not have stepped out of thought for a moment. Simply drop thought and the other is already there. You do not have to seek it, and there is no "becoming" in it.

Let us explore a section from the *Text* of *A Course In Miracles* entitled "Fear and Conflict."[7]

> *Being afraid seems to be involuntary; something beyond your own control. Yet I have said already that only constructive acts should be involuntary.*

Is fear involuntary? Are constructive acts involuntary? We have to ask ourselves these questions and find out. By so doing we will awaken other potentials within us. The questioning that is sincere and earnest has in it the power to bring us to the gaps between the thoughts that can receive. In that intensity of attention, the Given is made accessible.

> *My control can take over everything that does not matter, while my guidance can direct everything that does, if you so choose.*

What is the difficulty in our choosing to receive His help? Are we willing to experiment to see if what the Course is saying is true? Our acceptance cannot be of blind faith. We must bring our own energy into it and find out directly. Which is true: is fear involuntary, or are constructive thoughts involuntary?

> *Fear cannot be controlled by me, but it can be self-controlled.*

How inspiring and direct! Hearing this, would we still refuse to take responsibility for our own co-operation? Is fear not part of thought? Do we now see how essential it is to take a stand and no longer be ruled by thought?

...but it can be self-controlled.

How encouraging!

Fear prevents me from giving you my control.

As long as we are ruled by thought, which is fear, we are denying ourselves the help that is given and waiting to be received.

> *The presence of fear shows that you have raised body thoughts to the level of the mind. This removes them from my control, and makes you feel personally responsible for them. This is an obvious confusion of levels.*
>
> *I do not foster level confusion, but you must choose to correct it. You would not excuse insane behavior on your part by saying you could not help it. Why should you condone insane thinking? There is a confusion here that you would do well to look at clearly. You may believe that you are responsible for what you do, but not for what you think. The truth is that you are responsible for what you think, because it is only at this level that you can exercise choice. What you do comes from what you think.*

Can we appreciate the language of the Course? The precision and perfection of it? It is born out of such love.

> *What you do comes from what you think. You cannot separate yourself from the truth by "giving" autonomy to behavior. This is*

> *controlled by me automatically as soon as you*
> *place what you think under my guidance.*
> *Whenever you are afraid, it is a sure sign that*
> *you have allowed your mind to miscreate and*
> *have not allowed me to guide it.*

One of the factors of earth energies is that when fear comes in, we start projecting and we get busy with that. Fear is the means by which we get caught in illusion.

> *It is pointless to believe that controlling the*
> *outcome of mis-thought can result in healing.*
> *When you are fearful, you have chosen wrong-*
> *ly. That is why you feel responsible for it.*

Whenever we are afraid, we can be certain that our thoughts are miscreating. When we have the space to see that it may not be so, that it could all be illusion, miracles will begin to happen. Fear miscreates, but there is the power in us to question. The minute we start to question and put a stop to thought, God's help is already given. Without God's help we would not even question. See how swift the action is. We are not *waiting* for God's help, it is already given. If we realize the truth of this, we will be filled with exuberance knowing we are not alone.

> *You must change your mind, not your*
> *behavior, and this is a matter of willingness.*
> *You do not need guidance except at the mind*
> *level. Correction belongs only at the level*
> *where change is possible. Change does not*
> *mean anything at the symptom level, where it*
> *cannot work.*

The correction of fear is your responsibility. When you ask for release from fear, you are implying that it is not. You should ask, instead, for help in the conditions that have brought the fear about. These conditions always entail a willingness to be separate. At that level you can help it.

And what are the conditions in which fear exists?

You are much too tolerant of mind wandering...

Thought is the issue, is it not? And yet with greater energy and awareness, the mind can be brought to a stillness where the wandering ceases. No thought touches the mind that is still.

You are much too tolerant of mind wandering, and are passively condoning your mind's miscreations. The particular result does not matter, but the fundamental error does. The correction is always the same. Before you choose to do anything, ask me if your choice is in accord with mine.

What is it we ask for? Is it not for one activity versus another? "Should I go to San Francisco or to Denver?" Do we ever ask what His Will is independent of activity or preferences? When we ask Him, we have to step out of thought and listen to what He has to say. The problem is that we ask with thought and we do not have the space to give to receive His answer. We quickly conclude: "Well, I've waited long enough." We may even project an answer: "This is what the Lord told me. I'm going to San Francisco." It is unbelievable to see the deceptions that take place. We are so convinced about "my guide, my inner teacher, I'm channelling," and so forth.

> *Before you choose to do anything, ask me if your choice is in accord with mine. If you are sure that it is, there will be no fear.*

Make sure that when you ask you can overcome your own choice. That alone is quite a step. Then what *you* want to do does not control you. The minute you are outside of choice, you have taken the step. There is no time involved. That very instant the action has taken place that helps you to outgrow choice and to let go.

When you ask and there is no predetermined choice in your mind, have you not overcome thought already? No longer controlled by thought and its projections and choices, you are filled with gratefulness. You just cannot contain the joy of it. All choices are dissolved. When it is not "do this instead of that," "THY WILL BE DONE" becomes a reality.

> *Fear is always a sign of strain, arising whenever what you want conflicts with what you do. This situation arises in two ways: First, you can choose to do conflicting things, either simultaneously or successively. This produces conflicted behavior, which is intolerable to you because the part of the mind that wants to do something else is outraged. Second, you can behave as you think you should, but without entirely wanting to do so. This produces*

> *consistent behavior, but entails great strain. In*
> *both cases, the mind and the behavior are out*
> *of accord, resulting in a situation in which you*
> *are doing what you do not wholly want to do.*

We cannot just read this paragraph as a ritual. It has to be understood because it is a Law. If we read the Course with the determination to know, then we will know. By so doing, we have already called upon Other Forces to help us. Reading the Course in that way can bring about a total transformation in our lives.

A Course In Miracles offers us a different kind of thought — it is the Thought of God. It is full of love and compassion, and caressingly starts to show us that there is something that needs more attention. If we put our hearts into it, eventually we will find that we are co-creators. Our thought will no longer be of the manmade system of relative thinking; it will be related to His Thought. In that clarity, illusion is dissolved.

> *...the mind and the behavior are out of accord,*
> *resulting in a situation in which you are doing*
> *what you do not wholly want to do. This*
> *arouses a sense of coercion that usually*
> *produces rage, and projection is likely to follow.*

Projection is likely to follow — we can be certain of that. Do you see how clever we are? The brain has managed to exist for a long time.

> *Whenever there is fear, it is because you have*
> *not made up your mind. Your mind is therefore*

split, and your behavior inevitably becomes erratic. Correcting at the behavioral level can shift the error from the first to the second type, but will not obliterate the fear.

It is possible to reach a state in which you bring your mind under my guidance without conscious effort, but this implies a willingness that you have not developed as yet. The Holy Spirit cannot ask more than you are willing to do.

The Holy Spirit would not ask, but perhaps we could be more willing. Out of that, something else would grow.

The strength to do comes from your undivided decision. There is no strain in doing God's Will as soon as you recognize that it is also your own.

Would you believe that there is no strain in doing the Will of God?

The lesson here is quite simple, but particularly likely to be overlooked. I will therefore repeat it, urging you to listen. Only your mind can produce fear. It does so whenever it is conflicted in what it wants, producing inevitable strain because wanting and doing are discordant. This can be corrected only by accepting a unified goal.

The first corrective step in undoing the error is to know that the conflict is an expression of fear. Say to yourself that you must somehow have chosen not to love, or the fear could not have arisen. Then the whole process of correction becomes nothing more than a series of pragmatic steps in the larger process of accepting the Atonement as the remedy. These steps may be summarized in this way:

1. *Know first that this is fear.*
2. *Fear arises from lack of love.*
3. *The only remedy for lack of love is perfect love.*
4. *Perfect love is the Atonement.*

I have emphasized that the miracle, or the expression of Atonement, is always a sign of respect from *the worthy* to *the worthy. The recognition of this worth is re-established by the Atonement. It is obvious, then, that when you are afraid, you have placed yourself in a position where you need Atonement. You have done something loveless, having chosen without love.*

Is the discovery of this not a miracle? The minute we recognize we have done something loveless, a miracle would take place — especially if we do not keep on insisting on our own point of view. If it is just intellectual agreement, then no change has taken place and we will still find a lawyer to sue the other or justify our grievance.

This is precisely the situation for which the Atonement was offered. The need for the remedy inspired its establishment. As long as you recognize only the need for the remedy, you will remain fearful. However, as soon as you accept the remedy, you have abolished the fear. This is how true healing occurs.

Everyone experiences fear. Yet it would take very little right-thinking to realize why fear occurs. Few appreciate the real power of the mind, and no one remains fully aware of it all the time. However, if you hope to spare yourself from fear there are some things you must realize, and realize fully. The mind is very powerful, and never loses its creative force. It never sleeps. Every instant it is creating. It is hard to recognize that thought and belief combine into a power surge that can literally move mountains. It appears at first glance that to believe such power about yourself is arrogant, but that is not the real reason you do not believe it. You prefer to believe that your thoughts cannot exert real influence because you are actually afraid of them. This may allay awareness of the guilt, but at the cost of perceiving the mind as impotent. If you believe that what you think is ineffectual you may cease to be afraid of it, but you are hardly likely to respect it. There are no idle thoughts. All thinking produces form at some level.[8]

The world is trying to solve the problem of fear and anger in a loveless way. The greater the conflict, the greater the fear. The energy of the earth is being used for destruction rather than for what is constructive.

We are blessed that *A Course In Miracles* is given to us. If we bring it to application, then naturally we can no longer be part of the world and the quality of our being will have its own effect. We won't campaign "against" anything because that is part of conflict too. Two wrongs do not make a right. To be independent of thought, illusions, and influences, is to be who you are as God created you. That state cannot be touched by fear.

HE has told us we can take care of fear because we created it, we produced it, we projected it — therefore, we can undo it. It is an internal action of self-knowing that has nothing to do with the external. And that is all we have to do.

CHAPTER EIGHT

"Let every voice but God's be still in me."

"Father, today I would but hear Your Voice. In deepest silence I would come to You, to hear Your Voice and to receive Your Word. I have no prayer but this: I come to You to ask You for the truth. And truth is but Your Will, which I would share with You today."

Today we let no ego thoughts direct our words or actions. When such thoughts occur, we quietly step back and look at them, and then we let them go. We do not want what they would bring with them. And so we do not choose to keep them. They are silent now. And in the stillness, hallowed by His Love, God speaks to us and tells us of our will, as we have chosen to remember Him.

A Course In Miracles
Workbook For Students
Lesson 254, page 411

8

THE NEED
TO STEP OUT
OF THOUGHT

HAVE YOU EVER NOTICED that when you are silent even the sound of a car passing by is pleasing? The sound of the car does not bother you because you are not resisting it. Yet we spend most of our time and energy resisting things. What are we going to do with our resistances? We have invented good names for them and we pamper them as our likes and dislikes. But both are forms of resistance.

A Course In Miracles tells us that the external world is not real.

> *The world you see is an illusion of a world. God did not create it, for what He creates must be eternal as Himself.*[1]

> *What is this world?*
> *The world is false perception.*[2]

> *The world of time is the world of illusion.*[3]

In actuality, who you are is independent of what is external because the external is projected by the senses. The external does not exist, but it has reality to the physical senses. The physical senses are part of the gross, or dense, aspect of life. Let us explore this.

The physical body is gross and we have identified ourselves with it. Over the millennia we have become more and more preoccupied with the body as a separate entity. We have forgotten our true identity with the eternal and as a result live a life of isolation. Where there is isolation, there is always unfulfillment. It matters not whether the person is a king, a peasant, an economist, a scientist, whatever, if a person is isolated he does not have a sense of wholeness.

The body senses know nothing other than what is physical. And so, being subject to the laws of time, the physical body has gradually become very dense. What does that mean? It means the body has become extremely limited. It knows nothing other than self-centeredness. The senses of a gross, dense body can only see that which is gross and dense. It is impossible for it to see anything else. Therefore, it can never know contentment.

There are other levels in us, however, that are less dense than the body. Thought, for instance, is far more subtle than the body. It is not as limited as the body because it has its own expansion, but it is limited, nevertheless. First we are limited by the body, and then we are limited by thought with its ideologies and concepts, its beliefs and conditioning. That is what we live by whether we like it or not. We may *think* we are no longer part of religious dogma or addicted to nationality. That is what we *think*. But thought is very deceptive. We are addicted because thought itself is not our thought. Society conditions our thought and the past determines our values. Being influenced, we have no original thought of our own.

Can we see the limitation of thought? Thought will never trust what it does not know. How can the mental body trust God or love or peace? These are things thought has never known and therefore, it is convinced that there is no such thing as God, love, or peace. Do you know just how limited thought is? All bloodshed is caused by thought. Knowing this, do you still want to solve your problems using thought — which is, by definition, destructive? Would you put your trust in that?

Can we see also that we are bound to the body and its sensations? They regulate our eating habits and our sexual habits and everything else. We are addicted to sensation in one form or another. There are certain physical sensations the child does not know until he comes to puberty, but he has other sensations nonetheless. When you get older, certain sensations may drop away but then vanity and ambition come in. Sensations are not only physical, you know; they can also be, like greed or the attraction to status, of the mental body. They can be very powerful.

This is the nature of the world we live in. And into this world comes the child who is innocent. He does not know he is an American, an Eskimo, or an Indian. He is innocent and does not belong to anything yet. But we soon take care of that. In his innocence, the child reaches out to hold the dancing flames of a fire. As the child grows his innocence begins to disappear. We make sure he gets "educated" and the child becomes fearful and prejudiced. We give the child our fears as we train him to fit into society and into our concepts — the mental body. The child becomes increasingly addicted and insecure; then he has children and the pattern is repeated. This has gone on all through the ages.*

In the midst of our so-called "progress," universities have also come along to "educate" the child, and religious institutions to "enlighten" him. And so the child learns about Argentina or the Philippines or how bad Siberia is; and he adopts a religious thought system and becomes a Hindu, a Protestant, or a Catholic. But can thought eradicate fear? Has thought ever taken away hate? Can thought ever become that which is not of thought?

Where there is fear, there is hate. It is unavoidable. You cannot live in isolation and not have fear. And whatever you are afraid of, you will also hate. Thought makes sure of that.

We have a great responsibility to introduce the innocent child to wholeness rather than to our own fears, concepts, and prejudices. If the child becomes confused, vicious, or dogmatic, it is we who are

---

* For further discussions on the upbringing of children, see *How To Raise A Child Of God* by Tara Singh (Foundation for Life Action, 1987). (Editor)

responsible for it. But as long as we are still ruled by our thought, is it possible for us to be responsible?

Is there a religion that is based on wholeness and therefore excludes no one? What a marvelous religion that would be! No one is excluded in the Christ. The Christ state is the most subtle of states — it is not physical or mental. It knows no limitation but is a state of being in which all is One. When you become part of that state you too are part of the One. You could be Jewish or Moslem, but you would still be part of the One. This state is independent of the body and its thought system for it is part of the Oneness in which there is no separation. It is innocent of the ways of unreality and illusion.

To discover the Law of the One is the most wonderful thing that could happen to a human being. But what difference does it make to us to hear this? Would our thought ever allow us to know the Oneness of the Christ state?

To know the state of being that is Absolute — untouched by fear or hate — we *must* be free from thought. And, even though we may be constantly preoccupied, there is a state in which all seeking ends. Only when the seeking ends can one realize peace within the world of chaos.

When you can truthfully state, "I am not part of thought," there is no limitation. The blessing of that which is not of thought surrounds you and you say,

> *Today the peace of God envelops me,*
> *And I forget all things except His Love.*[4]

This is the ending of all seeking, all fear, all anxiety, all worry.

Soar beyond thought and you will see that there is love in the world. It is love that ends the seeking in each person. It is love that brings stability in a world of fear and insecurity. Not until man has ended all seeking will he know that he is independent of the external. Then his life becomes productive: he has dignity, poise, and virtue. He does not exploit another. The laws of virtue are not regulated by time, and are unknown to thought and the body senses.

> *Today the peace of God envelops me,*
> *And I forget all things except His Love.*

That is the state that makes resurrection possible in human life. It is a state superior to thought. There is no peace or love at the thought level. Thought merely projects the outer world of unreality and lives in that abstraction.

Can the mental body recognize that it is limited and isolated, and see that it knows no reality, no truth, no love, or peace? Seeing the obvious, it brings it to an end and becomes receptive. It receives that which is Given — therefore, it is not of thought or of the body. We must come to seriousness, to attention, to awareness, so that we can receive that which is not personal. It is possible.

We have been given *A Course In Miracles*. How many lifetimes we must have yearned for it! And now that it is here we cannot seem to heed it. Why? His words are here. He has said:

> *Nothing real can be threatened.*
> *Nothing unreal exists.*

If you are real, you will never be threatened. Why then do you want to stay in the unreal world of illusions? That is the world of thought. That which is real is not touched by thought. Do you see that there is an urgency for us to step out of thought?

The world is absolutely worn out by its education and its dogmas. Exhausted and dissipated, it cannot even receive peace.

Do we see what human beings are capable of doing: six million tons of bombs were dropped over Vietnam. We cannot depend on education or on anything external. We have to be responsible for our own integrity. And now all the help we need is given directly *to us* — *A Course In Miracles,* with its step-by-step curriculum.

Why doesn't it gladden our hearts? Why do we not want to sing songs of joy within ourselves and burn away the sorrow of the known? A new light has come to us, direct words of the Course that are Absolute Knowledge. What more could we want? Why is it we cannot bring anything to application? The Course says:

> *My thoughts do not mean anything.*[5]

And,

> *There is nothing to fear.*[6]

What would it take to stay with that until you know the truth of it? As long as you are preoccupied with ideas, you will know you are not serious. See yourself for what you are. But do not condemn yourself. There is already enough sorrow in our lives. Just see the fact of what is: that we are mediocre human beings not really interested in change, that we are prisoners of the known, constantly preoccupied with illusions, not knowing which way to turn. Even though we are given the Course — the direct Thoughts of God — we cannot give it the attention and, because we are dissipated, we cannot apply it.

Seeing the fact of this will free you from the mediocrity. Seeing the fact has no "becoming" in it. "Becoming" has not led man out of mediocrity. It but intensifies sorrow and brings more illusions.

See yourself just the way you are. Become a witness to yourself without judgment or condemnation. Just observe. And if you see yourself as mediocre, be at peace with it because in reality that is not who you are. It is the "becoming" that is mediocre, not you. Who you are is far superior to anything you could ever imagine.

Lesson 346 of the *Workbook* inspires us:

> *Today the peace of God envelops me,*
> *And I forget all things except His Love.*

> *Father, I wake today with miracles correcting my perception of all things. And so begins the day I share with You as I will share eternity, for time has stepped aside today. I do not seek*

the things of time, and so I will not look upon them. What I seek today transcends all laws of time and things perceived in time. I would forget all things except Your Love. I would abide in You, and know no laws except Your law of love. And I would find the peace which You created for Your Son, forgetting all the foolish toys I made as I behold Your glory and my own.

And when the evening comes today, we will remember nothing but the peace of God. For we would learn today what peace is ours, when we forget all things except God's Love.[7]

It is God's Love that makes forgetting possible. But we distrust love and we trust only our thought. That is the decision we have to make: either to trust love, or to trust thought.

> *Today the peace of God envelops me,*
> *And I forget all things except His Love.*

This lesson ends all seeking and brings one to a state of blessing. Then there is love to give and peace to impart to a tired world.

CHAPTER NINE

You cannot evaluate an insane belief system from within it. Its range precludes this. You can only go beyond it, look back from a point where sanity exists and see the contrast. Only by this contrast can insanity be judged as insane....

Lack of knowledge of any kind is always associated with unwillingness to know, and this produces a total lack of knowledge simply because knowledge is total.... The Holy Spirit judges against the reality of the ego's thought system merely because He knows its foundation is not true. Therefore, nothing that arises from it means anything. He judges every belief you hold in terms of where it comes from. If it comes from God, He knows it to be true. If it does not, He knows that it is meaningless.

A Course In Miracles
Text
page 164-165

9

THOUGHT
IS
INSANITY

IT MAY SEEM THAT the closer we get to *A Course In Miracles*, the further away we are from knowing it. The false build-up, the hopes, and deceptions get revealed; we see that half of us wants to change and the other half doesn't. And the half that does not want to change is quite content with the preoccupation of seeking and *believing* that it *wants* to.

Millions of people live under the pretense that they want to change. Becoming aware of this trap is quite a step. At least one misperception is being seen as a fact and therefore undone. Essentially, this misperception about "wanting to change" is the basis of all conflict. If one really saw this as a fact, something different would happen that is not born of conflict.

Shall we qualify what we mean by a "fact"? A fact is not something that is verbal. A fact is independent of thought. When we have seen something that is independent of thought, that seeing is called "vision." So far, however, we have only seen thought with its conclusions and "knowings" — and these are all part of illusion, part of a thinking that is contrary to God.

We have already gone into the nature of thinking quite a bit. We have seen that thought is made of conclusions, partial knowing, and the denial that we are already perfect. Our thinking is based on time and on "becoming." That is the fact of it. If you see this as fact, you will never be misled by your thought because you will have discovered that thoughts are not facts, thereby freeing yourself from the authority of thought.

Thought replaces God — a fact replaces thought and becomes vision. "Seeing the fact" means seeing something outside of thought. It is therefore vision that can never be clouded because its light and energy are with you forever. It does not come and go. It is unchangeable.

Thought is not interested in a fact because it manufactures its own projections. What thought calls a fact might be an admission that, "I don't like you and I am being true to myself by telling you exactly what I think." But do like and dislike have anything to do with fact?

We see that thought is a deviation from fact while a fact undoes thought. That is why we circumvent facts. We are deliberately determined to use thought. Why not change things around? Can we be determined to use fact instead?

Where does the difficulty lie? Is the difficulty not our unwillingness? Is there any problem other than unwillingness? Is our unwillingness an assumption that we cannot live without thought? Will unwillingness ever ask itself this question when it has all of thought at its disposal?

We are determined to use thought to solve problems. That means for the rest of our lives we will live by problems and seek solutions, and we will be victims of situations external to us. When we try to solve problems with thought, it is only a continuation of the problem. Why do we not admit that we are deliberately choosing to live a life subject to the externals, subservient to thought, having problems and seeking solutions? We are determined to live that way. We can deny it, but that is also a lie because it is of thought again.

Can you say one thing that is not of thought? What would that be? You see, we try to get to a fact through thought, but thought knows only problems and solutions. Is there ever a problem in a fact? The fact sees that only the misperception of thought projects problems. And you are determined to keep the problem and make it real. Your whole life is invested in it. Now someone asks, "Look, is that reasonable?" The challenge is placed before *you*. It is not abstract anymore.

As long as you are determined not to see the fact, you will continue thinking. And that is misperception because thought is not real. The fact is that thought is self-destructive. However, when you see the deception of thought, vision takes place. That is possible right now because the grace of God is upon you. How you make use of it determines who you are. Either you give up thought, or you give yourself up to the misery of thought and remain a victim of the world.

I am determined to see things differently.[1]

Are we beginning to see the importance of coming to this determination? So far, our determination has been to keep the illusions alive and, thus, maintain the authority thought has over us. That is deliberate too.

How does one heal misperception? By seeing the fallacy of the thought by which we are determined to live! We always have determination; it is just misdirected.

The words "deliberate" and "determined" mean something you do consciously. If you consciously choose to live by thought, please recognize that thought is ever in duality — it contradicts itself. Thought itself *is* a contradiction. It can believe it wants to change, but underneath it is always determined to be thought and so it does not change. We will say, "I want God," as long as it is the god of thought.

The minute we are shown the fallacy of thought, we become helpless and say, "I don't know what to do." If that were true — that we *really* didn't know what to do — we would not go to thought again.

Humility does not depend on thought, helplessness does.

The question remains: why are we determined to live by thought and its problem-seeking solutions? Can we see the insanity of it? What are we doing about our own insanity? It is not something outside of us. Unless we clearly see this, we will not bring the insanity to healing. And the purpose of *A Course In Miracles* is healing.

What weakness is there in each one of us that needs to be corrected? Can we see the fact that there is rightness in healing our own misperceptions? The system is not going to do it. But we, as individuals, can and must. Society can justify its insanity and say that love is no longer necessary upon the planet; it can justify its insecurity and fear, its selfishness, and its obsession with self-survival that depends on skills. Yet it is a very convenient fallacy to think that only the big banks and insurance companies promote this insane system. We are part of insanity too. Healing misperception must begin in our own lives.

Could you take one thing on in yourself that needs to be corrected? You could also select one virtue you would like to live up to. You must make sure, however, that your willingness is not unwillingness in disguise. There is an inherent unwillingness in us that always *believes* it is willing. There are many such deceptions we will discover, and in the discovery of them we will also see that the insanity is not outside of us. Self-centeredness and selfishness are not external. They are within us. And these are the things we must change.

Can you also recognize that as long as your mind is pressured with fear, anxiety, greed, ambition, or whatever, it cannot really relate with anything? We are pressured by our "knowings," by our unwillingness, by our problems. Man is pressured and, consequently, produces a pressured environment of abuse, exploitation, and corruption.

Yet, in the midst of all this, there are Other Forces we can call upon. If we came to something called faith and trust, we could make contact with the grace of God. Do we ever give thanks to the Lord for His many blessings — not with yesterday's stale words, but with the newness of each moment? Real gratefulness is always new. It never becomes a routine or ritual. Gratefulness is not born out of pressure, it is born out of a fact, out of reality.

A fact has inherent in it an urgency. Does urgency have pressure? Have you ever considered these things in a deep way? Is there pressure in urgency?

When you have urgency, you could be in the midst of chaos and disaster, but your mind would still be clear and undisturbed. When you are pressured you are confused, are you not? You do not know what to do; you panic and get lost. You might be looking for your keys everywhere, all the while having them right in your pocket.

Urgency relies on fact; pressure relies on thought. When you have urgency, the intensity of awareness widens the gaps between the thoughts and you remain alert and efficient. When you are pressured, thought is activated even more than usual and leads to fear and panic. It becomes more and more insane without even knowing it.

Do you see how responsible each person has to be? And how important it is to bring order to our lives and minds? What is that responsibility? What is that challenge?

The human brain is very sensitive and energetic. It has the capacity to come to such energy that it can touch upon and make contact with something far more powerful and glorious than itself, which is the Mind.

This inherent potential within the brain, however, can also get distracted and thereby become insane and destructive. Life is One, but a slack brain projects "another," something opposite to it. It then wants, pursues, is suspicious, hates. This is how the deception of separation takes place in the brain.

When the energy of the brain is not dissipated, it comes closer to its own nature of sensitivity and energy and functions most efficiently. Functioning with this kind of energy, it moves towards love rather than fear. When the energy of the brain is contained, it moves away from distraction, desires, and wanting. That is the beginning of intelligence. The brain comes to a kind of wholeness which is aware of the Mind, something very vast. The brain with its thought no longer moves; it becomes attentive. It becomes aware of that Mind which is One. And nothing is outside of it. There is no separation in it; therefore, it knows no fear. It simply knows nothing other than perfection, order, and glory.

This is the responsibility: to bring the mind to a sensitivity that knows no fear, no problems, and no insecurity. In this state, we become aware of the One Mind of which we are all a part. Out of that, some other Action takes place that we cannot name because it is not of the brain. But it will be given, and we will extend it.

God created One Son in His Own Likeness, unlimited and timeless. When the brain has gathered itself and is fully sensitive and alive — therefore totally still — it realizes there is no "other." Love exists, and no one is outside of it. It is the love of the Father for His Son, and the love of the Son for His Father.

But once the brain loses that intensity, that aware-ness, that contact with the Mind — it separates. It projects a "you" and a "me." The One Son has become a billion sons and they go on multiplying. But they cannot live together because each one is thinking about himself. Eons upon eons the same pattern repeats. That is the movement of time versus timelessness.

This separation becomes reality for us. And because we continue to confirm that separation exists, our relationship with one another is one of exploitation, gratification, and fear. There is always somebody about whom we have an opinion. He has his; we have ours. But they are just images. They are not real at all. This is called insanity!

Insanity only knows to strengthen its own greed, its own fear, and its own attachment. What are we going to do to heal the insanity in each one of us? There is no need to blame ourselves or anyone else. This may be what we have made of ourselves, but it is not who we really are.

There is a prayer in *A Course In Miracles* that states:

I will be healed as I let Him teach me to heal.[2]

There is only one healing. It is not physical. Healing is of one's mind — the mind is healed of its misperception.

In the understanding of the insanity is the correction. Healing takes place in seeing the fact as the fact. And the challenge of this becomes a most beautiful gift of God to you. You are grateful for having seen it. That which showed it to you is with you; it is part of you. And you will not be defeated. All we need is trust. We need faith that there are Other Forces beyond the appearances. Appearances divide; trust and faith unite.

I can assure you that if you could know these two things, everything would be healed. No worry or fear would ever touch you.

I am as God created me.[3]

I rest in God.[4]

You are not alone. Knowing this, how can one contain one's appreciation! Knowing this, you are linked with the grace of God that heals the human brain. It is an action of faith in the absolute words of the Course rather than trust in insanity. That action is the stillness of trust and faith versus the movement of insanity. It is an Action that is of Life. The power of this faith is so strong that nothing of the earth can ever affect you. It simply cannot. Can we come to valuing trust? Can we heed? The power behind these two statements would give you its strength. As long as you remember it, it would impart its strength to you. There is nothing you need to do except to have that faith.

I rest in God is for those who have "the ears to hear" and who see the falseness of the activity of the brain. When the brain is not making contact with the Mind it cannot know the Action of Grace. Then whatever it does out of separation is insane, self-centered, and fearful.

If you really heard the truth of this, what would it do to you? Can you see how essential it is for us to know, as a fact, that when the brain moves it is confused, and its movement does not know love or truth? If that fact was established, would it not heal insanity? It would have its effect irrespective of all "doings." Just the awareness of the unreality of the activity of the brain could revolutionize your life.

Action, then, can only be one of ending, of undoing. And that is the decision we have to make — to end the activity of insanity in ourselves because we are responsible for it. What honesty will we now give to our lives?

I rest in God.

Has this now become our faith, our truth? Or has it remained an ideal? You see, the inherent unwillingness in us can be trained and converted and influenced at the brain level, and it will agree to nice ideas. But the actuality and the living of truth is quite a different matter. It is in the stepping out of insanity where the unwillingness lies. And we have not yet deviated from insanity.

What is it in us that refuses to see that we do not want to change? We make believe we do and we deceive ourselves in order to maintain our insanity. Insanity and deception are all part of a package deal called unwillingness. We may not be able to truthfully say, *I rest in God,* but we *can* say that we deceive ourselves. Now what will we do with this truth — with the awareness of the fact that everything we do is a lie and a deception, a part of insanity?

Now we can see the importance of self-knowledge. Self-knowing is not abstract idealism that always wants an "opposite." Self-knowing comes from observation of what is recognized as fact. And this can be expressed. Self-knowing observes thought and speaks of what thought is. This observation can be called awareness — an awakening that is independent of thought. In self-knowing is the awareness that is not of thought.

Awareness has some other Action in it that thought cannot know because it is not limited and does not have an "opposite." Awareness is pure energy without conflict. It is a light that awakens in you. It cannot contain itself, for it naturally needs to express. And how does it express?

It expresses what it has seen of truth and therefore enriches us all. Awareness is the sharing of what it is: something profound that is not of thought. It extends to all brothers the gift of clarity, which is far superior to thought.

The action that is not of the brain is the action of awareness that undoes. It ends the activity of thought that is based on insecurity, fear, and doubt. Awareness brings us to the truth of:

I rest in God.

And,

I am as God created me.[5]

Thought cannot. When it becomes your reality, something extraordinary has happened upon the planet. One person who would not pursue projections and separation has come to resurrection. This is a vital step that, sooner or later, each person will have to take.

CHAPTER TEN

Sit quietly and look upon the world you see, and tell yourself: "The real world is not like this. It has no buildings and there are no streets where people walk alone and separate. There are no stores where people buy an endless list of things they do not need. It is not lit with artificial light, and night comes not upon it. There is no day that brightens and grows dim. There is no loss. Nothing is there but shines, and shines forever."

A Course In Miracles
Text
page 236

10
THE PRESSURES
ON MANKIND

THE PROBLEMS OF MAN TODAY have accelerated almost to a breaking point. And there is very little anyone can do. There is so much stress upon each one. Whether it is education, the family situation, or having a job, everything contributes to putting more and more pressure on the human brain. It is quite obvious that the mind of the age is under a great deal of pressure.

When the mind is pressured, it is almost incapable of wisdom. Yet it would be difficult for man to be controlled if he were wise. Wisdom, however, does not seem to be a need of this age. It is not needed by our present educational system or by our highly technological lifestyle. Nor is wisdom needed in the commercialized life of man who, not having his own work, is subject to a job and lives in an artificial environment, unrelated to nature or to the early hours of the morning.

What is this stress about? Is the stress related to how you make a living? One of the first questions people ask when one comes to the West from a different culture is: "How do you make a living?" You would have to be very wise to hear the tyranny of these words. "How do you make a living?" It is only when we cannot identify with another as an individual, that we superficially ask this question.

To have a job is to be a mercenary. Yet a job is what is needed to support the commercialized lifestyle. The job requires skills that accelerate the activity of the day. It needs routine to function. But it is not in need of wisdom because wisdom emerges out of simplicity. The fruit of wisdom is simplicity — what you can do without rather than what you project and want.

Each person must question, "What is it that pressures me?" To answer this we must first see one simple thing: how much energy one single desire consumes. What havoc it plays! How it pressures the human brain! What are we obsessed with today? Is it not with things we want to buy? We are told what clothing styles to wear and everything else we need in order to keep pace with progress and the times.

More and more, desire and its gratification have become an obsession with man. Desire is the lowest form of energy. And desire multiplies desire. It is an inner corruption that puts man to sleep. We live in a myriad of endless desires which dissipate our energy.

Desire is the opposite of wisdom and simplicity. When we have desires, we do not have our own mind.

If we had our own mind, the externals could not intrude upon us. Man today is constantly being lured and therefore, controlled externally. We personalize life and isolate ourselves when we project desires and pursue them. And once we are isolated, we make good customers. We become more and more dependent on the externals when there is little contact with the harmony and gladness within.

How much energy we expend to sustain our desires! In order to produce and manufacture the objects of our desire, we have to labor. It makes of us a slave. We need a job to have money to buy the things that satisfy those desires. Under stress, the tendency is to want to get away from it all. This produces the need for outlets and therefore, distractions and indulgences have become very important.

Today it seems inconceivable to live a life without the pressure of desires. But is desire itself necessary? It would take a great deal of wisdom to confront and question desire. Is desire necessary in a God-created world of perfection, of completeness?

Would the things we desire have meaning in an honest life or a life of wisdom? The wise would value stillness rather than distractions, forms of escape, and indulgences. He would be totally free of these pressures. We, on the other hand, decorate our limitations and take false pride in beliefs that add to our pressured lives. Can the belief that we are an American or a Navajo or a Mexican be true?

We are human beings. And the human being is one who has his own mind, his own space, his own radiance. He is not limited to the body, nor to time. Would we need cocktail hours then? Would we be news-mongers? Would we know separation?

Have you ever questioned this way? Do you have any space at all of your own to question? Having a pressured mind means you have no space of your own. We need to see that man has lost his space. He works in an office without a space of his own, for the most part. If he owns a house, the expenses and taxes are so high that it is no longer really his own. We do not have fruit-bearing trees that are our own, nor do we have our own water. We do not even have our own thought.

There is very little space in this daily life of pressured existence. In our quest to accomplish more, the state of stillness that has the energy to dispel any intrusion from the external is almost totally taken away.

This original space within you that is your own is the strength that external artificiality cannot affect. What a being he must be who has his own space — an unpressured space within the brain that cannot be intruded upon!

Talking about stepping out of the pressures is of no use. It must be something *you* explore. In the exploring, you can discover something that is not pressured, something that is independent of thought. You must find the integrity and the love of self-honesty within *you* that nothing external can intrude upon. Otherwise, you will still be influenced by another and remain subject to the laws of time.

Society today, more than ever before, is regulated by the clock. If you were truly honest to yourself, you would demand of yourself that you be independent of these pressures and of conformity. Then whatever you would do would be essential. It would carry its own space.

Integrity does not conform to anything external or to any belief system. It is true to itself. Yet integrity is probably the hardest thing for us to come to. At the same time, it is the most natural and the easiest thing to do. If you find it difficult — which you will — you will also discover how conditioned your brain is, how programmed you are, and how little space there is within the brain for the *new* to be.

You will also find out directly what pressure is, for the discovery itself will introduce you to other potentials within. Discovery is an individual thing that has the power to question and the power to undo. In discovery, you realize that there is something more than time and belief systems.

Each person *must* come to his own discovery, for within each one of us there is a light. We are children of light, not darkness. First, discover that you stand in darkness without a mind of your own, without your own honesty. When you realize the light that you are, nothing in the world will be able to touch you with pressures or external values.

Nothing real can be threatened.
Nothing unreal exists.

Discover the truth of this and you will be freed from all pressures. Pressures prevent us from knowing what is real. But are pressures part of life? Or are they part of thought? Again, we must ask: "What is thought?" Thought is the breeding ground of insecurity, fear, and desires. Thought knows only lack. Thought itself is a pressure and we have trained thought with skills.

Nothing that is part of creation is ever pressured. The tree is not pressured, nor are the birds. Only man's brain is pressured and therefore, he is getting more and more dull, more and more self-destructive. The worst is yet to come. We have known the efficiency of fear and the efficiency of greed. We have yet to discover the efficiency of vengeance.

The faster the pace, the more self-destructive we become. This is quite obvious. We have less time to eat the right food or to be with the rhythm of Life. Divine leisure is a lost concept. The twilight hour when we should be still is when we want to get down to a sub-level and have cocktails or watch television. More activity. Countless outlets have been invented to help us escape from the pressure.

We are always with the movement of thought. And the movement of thought has become so accelerated there is no space for anything else. Can we see that more demands are made on us, whether it is speed reading or faster jets to get us places quicker? Even if we sit quiet we get bored. Why must we always be doing something? Thought drives us from one activity to another: we watch a movie, look at magazines, read a book, or even, take a tranquilizer.

The pressure on the brain is produced by fear, insecurity, and projected desires, and it must find its escape by bringing the person to sub-level within. The brain does not rise to stillness where, having done its daily work, it can now be at leisure. And it degenerates even more when the way a man makes a living is false or what he produces is artificial.

Our educational system, television and radio programs, books, and magazines, all shape our mind and intrude upon our brain. What is the result of this influence? We are being schooled for survival. We form opinions about people we have never seen, and inevitably, wars result. Is this necessary? Do we need to be afraid of people we have not even met? Do we need to have an opinion about them or be regulated by them? We are becoming more and more divided. Fragmentation — not wholeness — is on the increase.

A pressured brain can never know what sanity is, for sanity is of a still mind. What would it be to come to a still mind and not be pressured? You would have to know yourself. You would have to weed out the unessentials in your life. You would need discrimination to see the false as the false. You may think you have discrimination if you choose a blue dress instead of a green one, but that is just a choice. Discrimination requires enormous energy. But the brain's energy is being dissipated.

Again, we must point out: your first responsibility as a human being is to know yourself. To know yourself you will have to outgrow nationalism and end the fragmentation and isolation in your life. That is the responsibility you must assume so that you can enter into a state of wholeness, where you sort out the real from the unreal, the essential from the unessential.

There would be no wars in the world if we were responsible. Ask yourself, to what do you give your energy? It is your responsibility to find out. Otherwise, whatever you do under pressure will have its consequences — and rather disastrous consequences at that. If you cannot be true to yourself, neither will you be true to your friends, your relatives, or to nature. Your sleep will not be sleep and your work will not be work because you will be acting out of pressure. Only survival will have importance to you in a world that is full of grace and the perfection of creation.

Being pressured, we will never know what love or truth is. We will never know what is eternal, nor will we know true relationship with our brother or with our Creator.

Unless man is related to internal life, he will always be pressured. Is any one of us related to that which is not of time, to that which is real? Even our gods are products of our thoughts. And thought, we as have seen, is conditioned and programmed.

Our knowing is limited to the past and to a projected future. The past has nothing to offer but fear. The past projects a future which is just like the past. When will we have enough of our yesterdays?

We have lost the discovery of the present moment. Yet only the present moment is real and unpressured by time because it is eternal. Why is it we choose to evade the present and remain victims of the fear of past and future?

In the present there is no threat. The present is protected for it is of God. There is only the NOW.

> *Nothing real can be threatened.*
> *Nothing unreal exists.*

This is the state of the NOW. Nothing external can intrude upon it. NOW is an extension of that which is real, that which is not of time. The NOW is what sets us free from the externals, from pressures, from fear.

Nothing real can be threatened is an Eternal Law. Without this direct contact with the eternal — of which we are already a part — invariably we must remain under the pressure of time. Where there is the pressure of time, each person wants to get the better of the other. Then you can be exploited, and you can exploit. Loss and gain, war and peace, become the way of life.

Nothing that God created can be threatened. Can we accept the truth of this? It would require putting away all desires, all insecurities, all pressures.

Everything in creation exists to help us. NOW is the time to call upon our strength and discover our reality. Nothing real can be affected by what is external. Things that are manmade come and go. Where is the Roman Empire today? But the Son of

God is eternal. The Son of God comes to the earth and affects what is of time with his eternity.

That is our function, for that is who we are. Freed from the pressure of time, we need no longer be afraid of anything external and we will have peace to impart to another.

> *Fear is not of the present, but only of the past and future, which do not exist. There is no fear in the present when each instant stands clear and separated from the past, without its shadow reaching out into the future. Each instant is a clean, untarnished birth, in which the Son of God emerges from the past into the present. And the present extends forever.*[1]

CHAPTER ELEVEN

"I can be hurt by nothing but my thoughts."

*"....When I think that I am hurt in any way,
it is because I have forgotten who I am, and that
I am as You created me. Your Thoughts can
only bring me happiness. If ever I am sad or
hurt or ill, I have forgotten what You think, and
put my little meaningless ideas in place of
where Your Thoughts belong, and where they
are. I can be hurt by nothing but my thoughts.
The Thoughts I think with You can only bless.
The Thoughts I think with You alone are true."*

A Course In Miracles
Workbook For Students
Lesson 281, page 428

11

"I CAN BE HURT
BY NOTHING
BUT MY THOUGHTS"

TRUTH IS ACCESSIBLE where there is attention. Attention is absolutely essential. When thought interferes, we begin to doubt and problems begin. Doubt brings confusion, lack of direction, and fear. It isolates us and we forget who we are. Then we think we are bodies and the external world of fear, selfishness, and insecurity becomes very real to us.

The origin of this world we see — a world that is brutal, tyrannical, and devoid of love — is doubt. If we had trust, there would be no such problem at all. But trust is a difficult thing. Can we see, then, that the issue is a matter of choice between trust and doubt? It can be that simple. And you and I must make the decision in our lives to be with doubt or with trust.

If you are with trust, the illusions of doubt no longer have sway over you. If you are with doubt, that is your reality and you will settle for belief in flags, nationalities, and religious dogmas. For the person who chooses doubt, fear becomes the basis of his life.

Again, fear has many names — survival, insecurity, doubt, and others. While we may understand this intellectually, the very intellectuality is also based on fear. Whatever we hear, we interpret. We cannot say that we have ever deeply understood anything in the true sense. Having an understanding that is direct is what is meant by having "the ears to hear."

A Course In Miracles points out:

I can be hurt by nothing but my thoughts.[1]

Could we insist upon knowing this? "My thoughts" cannot do anything but project fear. Can we look at thought that way? Thought is an invention of man that came into being after the separation took place. It is obsessed with survival and with "me first." And the "me" we know is a body that grows old and dies. Beyond the sensations of the body, we hardly know a thing.

I can be hurt by nothing but my thoughts.

Why not take on discovering the truth of this lesson and be determined to stay with it no matter what? If you did, could you ever be confused about what to do? The *Manual For Teachers* tells us:

> *The teachers of God have trust in the world, because they have learned it is not governed by the laws the world made up. It is governed by a Power That is in them but not of them. It is this Power That keeps all things safe. It is*

> *through this Power that the teachers of God*
> *look on a forgiven world.*[2]

The Bible points out something very similar. Jesus asserts that no matter what the dangers are — no matter if you are going to be persecuted, punished, or hated — if you would not lose faith or let fear enter into you, when the time of trial came, He would give you the words to speak.[3] No one could touch you.

But our thought is still going to project all kinds of fear, isn't it? Are you wise enough to see the deception of thought? It takes sanity to see what thought is.

Hard times may come in the world. It is natural that they do, because we are ruled by fear. But if we did not have fear, would we care whether times were difficult or easy?*

Christ said, "Don't worry about tomorrow. Tomorrow will take care of itself."[4] Will you let tomorrow take care of itself? If you had trust, could anything disturb you? How can you be threatened by the world and its unreality when you are not a part of it? That which is true, is true no matter how much you try to disguise it. If you live with rightness, there are no consequences. If your life is productive and intrinsic, problems cannot touch you because you are not part of the manmade world of illusions.

We have very little remembrance of anything eternal that is direct. We *want* to remember, but we do

---

* For further discussion of probable future events, see "The Future Of Mankind" in *The Future Of Mankind — The Branching Of The Road* by Tara Singh (Foundation for Life Action, 1986), pages 5-19. (Editor)

not see that wanting, itself, is born out of weakness and fear; that it is part of thought, not conviction. We cannot seem to come to a total transformation in our lives. We have lost faith in ourselves. There is very little integrity left at all.

What if you did not have food to eat for a few days and the landlord asked you to leave? What would you do? That would be real to you, would it not? But you would never see that you brought it upon yourself because you believe in consequences. You must not have lived rightly. We do not want to see what mistakes, oversights, and false values we have lived by, under the illusion that we are holy and righteous. Would you have the courage to be honest with yourself? Could you take a good look at your life and see where you have been irresponsible, wasteful, casual? Who will correct it if you don't? You will probably become very frightened — but it is your own thoughts that hurt you all along.

The thought that prevents you from coming to trust and integrity, to rightness and virtue, to truth and love, to forgiveness and non-judgment, to non-attack — is the same thought that brings about consequences, is it not? That thought is of your own making and so it can be said that you bring the consequences upon yourself. Could you, even in the throes of consequences and difficulties, say to yourself: "I know it will be difficult, but I will not fear even if I die"? By what conviction are you going to live?

Do you have trust in:

I am sustained by the Love of God ?[5]

Or that your only function is the one God gave you?[6] The Course says it in many different ways. Do you have the conviction that nothing external can affect whether you succeed or fail? Can you say you will never deviate into thought or believe that your thoughts are real?

To do so, you must call upon something more powerful than thought. It is called trust and it never ceases to see the world of thought as unreal. Unless there is that strength, the fluctuations between trust and doubt will continue.

Thought *is* doubt. It is self-centered and survival-oriented. To thought, success is important, not ethics. Neither are forgiveness and gratefulness, rightness and non-judgment, nor love and truth important to thought. It is quite simple.

You *must* go through that fire of purification that outgrows thought. No one can do it for you. *You* have to take a stand. It is *you* who distrusts, has fear, and projects doubts. Doubt is something *you* maintain. But trust is also something you can maintain. Which would you choose?

Can you use words that are valid? Or, are you going to answer these questions with wishful thinking, being influenced by another? We have to go *beyond* the word and come to the strength of the word. Can you feel the strength behind the words of a man who can say, "Doubt and fear are a stranger to me," and mean it? That man knows the law of grace. The power of the earth does not touch him.

> *Your doubts are meaningless, for God is certain. And the Thought of Him is never absent…. This course removes all doubts which you have interposed between Him and your certainty of Him.*

> *We count on God, and not upon ourselves, to give us certainty…. His sureness lies beyond our every doubt. His Love remains beyond our every fear. The Thought of Him is still beyond all dreams and in our minds, according to His Will.[7]*

Can there be anything more meaningful than to know:

> *I am sustained by the Love of God ?*

If thought regulates you, you are unable to love or be honest, and you remain a victim of fear. Yet,

> *I can be hurt by nothing but my thoughts.*

No one else can hurt you because, in actuality, there *is* no one else. In truth, there is only you. And you are the light of the world. The world needs that one light — and you have not accepted it.

We must come to conviction and determination. Each one of us can say, "I am not that light, but I will not remain insane either. I have now understood:

> *I can be hurt by nothing but my thoughts.*

And,

> *I will not be afraid of love today."[8]*

Will you live by and honor that? Can you take such an oath? This is not a favor you are doing for someone else — it is for *you*. Is it possible for you to say something you will honor, that time cannot affect? That you have taken a stand against illusions? Can you say, "I will never deviate from the strength these lessons impart:

I can be hurt by nothing but my thoughts.

I will not be afraid of love today. ?"

Do you realize that you could never make these statements unless He was already there with you? We can say things of time which do not last, but to say, "Until my dying day," would require that His blessing be upon us.

In actuality, one is not afraid *of* love, but afraid *to* love. If you have a car accident, you may *want* to love, but you are thinking more about your car: how much damage has been done, who is going to pay for it, and so forth. We are taught to calculate and therefore, are afraid to love.

Most of our fear is of calculation and loss, isn't it? Can we heed the words of Jesus when he said, "AND IF ANY MAN... TAKE AWAY THY COAT, LET HIM HAVE THY CLOAK ALSO"?[9] Attachment brings about defensiveness and fear. But when you say you will not be afraid to love, it also means you will not be attached. And that can take place within you.

Your commitment to love will either make you extremely wise or make a liar of you. If you are sincere and your words are true, it will change your whole thought system. If it is not true, you will start to calculate and you will soon discover what you "love" most. But, by learning how corrupt and uncaring thought really is, you could then become a light unto yourself! Isn't that beautiful?

Love and trust are not of the earth. When you can still love the person who offends, insults, or cheats you, you are already outside of time. Then your own thoughts will no longer frighten you and bring you down to the level of insanity. That is the meaning of, "IN GOD WE TRUST."[10]

Though miracles surround us, have we ever felt the need of them? We have wanted miracles to serve us, to "get things." Now we need them to correct misperception and to bring us to trust in God under *all* circumstances. This is what is needed to be at peace within. "I have come to conviction. I am ready." That determination would do wondrous things.

The One Who is an incarnation of love and peace will teach you, for you have laid your life in His hands.

I am sustained by the Love of God.

When this lesson is already in application in your life, it will bring about a cleansing because He will correct all misperceptions. "Wanting" to bring it to application is a reaction because thought itself is a reaction. We can make reaction very fanatic, but it is not trust. Trust has no thought in it.

Trust must be in application so that nothing can make you defensive or reactive, and therefore, fearful. You will then correct thoughts of fear, "wanting," and attack within yourself. Only then is there the possibility of being one with the Will of God.

> ...*love without trust is impossible, and doubt and trust cannot coexist.*[11]

To have trust is to be part of God's Plan for Salvation. It is His Plan. Let it be His, and He will bless you.

CHAPTER TWELVE

"Peace to my mind.
Let all my thoughts be still."

"Father, I come to You today to seek the peace
that You alone can give. I come in silence. In
the quiet of my heart, the deep recesses of my
mind, I wait and listen for Your Voice. My
Father, speak to me today. I come to hear Your
Voice in silence and in certainty and love, sure
You will hear my call and answer me."

Now do we wait in quiet. God is here, because
we wait together. I am sure that He will speak
to you, and you will hear. Accept my
confidence, for it is yours. Our minds are
joined. We wait with one intent; to hear our
Father's answer to our call, to let our thoughts
be still and find His peace, to hear Him speak
to us of what we are, and to reveal Himself unto
His Son.

A Course In Miracles
Workbook For Students
Lesson 221, page 392

12

"I AM UNDER NO LAWS BUT GOD'S" — A COMMENTARY

THE FIRST STEP in reading the lesson is to see if one truly understands, *I am under no laws but God's*.[1] Is our understanding intellectual, is it just verbal? Most probably that is what it is. Then, what is the fact of that? The fact is, we have made this truth — that *I am under no laws but God's* — into an abstract idea. We are constantly doing that, and we call it "learning." In fact, this kind of learning is more dangerous than not learning. As Thoreau said, "Natural ignorance has its place. But educated ignorance is a very dangerous thing."

I am under no laws but God's.

That is a truth. And almost everyone, with very few exceptions, will say, "I don't know the truth of it." And very few, if any, would understand that they make it into an abstract idea. Would you have known the truth of it, that you were making it abstract all the time?

We must first begin to see that we know nothing other than ideas. We are probably not interested in going any further, nor do we even think that there *is* anything further. We just say, "Well, I wish a miracle would happen." A person can have ten PhD's, but what difference would that make? The lesson is still of relative knowledge. And the main function of relative knowledge is to keep the separation intact.

Observe how we evade the Eternal Laws of God. We evade the God-created Self that knows no time and does not acknowledge illusions as real.

To be consistent with, *I am under no laws but God's*, we must undo the illusion of past and future. The first lessons of the Course dissolve the misperceptions of illusions, all self-projected beliefs, concepts, and dogmas. One is as if cleansed of distortions and the fallacy of make-believe.

> *Nothing I see... means anything.*[2]
> *I do not understand anything I see...*[3]
> *I see only the past.*[4]
> *My thoughts do not mean anything.*[5]

The fact is that these lessons undo and set one free. We need to bring the illusions of time to attention and to truth, so that they can be dispelled. We will soon discover that attention and interest effortlessly come upon miracles and holy instants. The capacity to receive miracles is awakened by seeing the fact as a fact.

Now let us discover the fact that there is no time. How quickly one's own energy of attention sees that we are always bringing the past "knowings" of memory into the present. Thus we never get to the boundless, creative vitality of the present in which there is no time at all. We must realize and recognize the truth of this, not intellectually, but actually. Actuality alone is true. It is free of the past and nothing external can intrude upon it.

Instantly one sees how the past overshadows, or, is ever over-shadowing the present. And when the holy instant remains hidden in the so-called future, the future too becomes the extension of the past. The fact is, one seldom steps out of the past. What you were — or assumed that you were — you remain. The same "you" remains because no transformation took place. One is still caught in the illusion of verbal "knowings."

I see only the past.[6]
My mind is preoccupied with past thoughts.[7]
My thoughts do not mean anything.[8]

Every single lesson of the Course offers salvation. Can we know the glory and wonder of just these three lessons? What wisdom and light there is inherent in them to liberate us. You will see for yourself there is no time or fear in eternity.

Fear will not intrude upon the glorious intensity of a timeless state of being. *I am under no laws but God's* means that, in the laws of God, there is no fear. Therefore, whenever we are afraid or insecure, we must then question ourselves, "Is this something I am projecting?"

The minute we see that fear is an illusion we are projecting, we have taken on a responsibility to do something about it. God has nothing to do with it, truth has nothing to do with it, and reality has nothing to do with it — we see that we are the ones who are doing it.

Our responsibility is to welcome and invite correction. When we bring correction, miracles happen. We have wanted miracles to happen in all kinds of things. But they do not just happen. The Holy Spirit's only function is to bring man to Atonement, to the ending of separation. He is not interested in the abstract, in self-improvement, or in "learning." The Holy Spirit is only interested in *undoing.* The primary purpose of *A Course In Miracles* — and that of any genuine teacher throughout the ages — is to undo.

The *Text* of the Course states:

> *The Holy Spirit leads you steadily along the path of freedom, teaching you how to disregard or look beyond everything that would hold you back.*[9]

A miracle is not affected by thought. In fact, a miracle makes thought non-effective. It requires a miracle, or insight, to see the falseness of thought. But we want to assert the authority of thought, the "knowings" of thought. The Course, on the other hand, through the Holy Spirit, corrects and undoes thought.

Now we have read only the title of this lesson. Can we see how much is demanded of us to come to the truth of the absolute words of the Course?

We have observed before how many senseless things have seemed to you to be salvation.

Has anyone observed that? We then would have to say, "I have not observed that." Do you think someone would say that? Without this kind of self-honesty, there is a lack of seriousness. The Course is not for the casual. When we are casual, we want someone to improve our casualness, and there is no interest in inner correction.

The Course deals with salvation. Can anyone come to salvation without realizing and recognizing the fact that, *I am under no laws but God's* ? Otherwise, we will always be preoccupied with our own projections. And what is manmade has no reality; it is merely illusion and projection.

...how many senseless things have seemed to you to be salvation. Each has imprisoned you with laws as senseless as itself.

Now, would we say that everything we know has imprisoned us?

Do you think anybody knows how to read the Course? Do you think there is a possibility someone could get interested? All of our "knowings" have imprisoned us, but the Course tells us:

> *You are not bound by them. Yet to understand*
> *that this is so, you must first realize salvation*
> *lies not there.*

But we are not totally interested in salvation. That is not our *single purpose.* If we were interested in salvation, we would know that we are imprisoning ourselves. How many people do you think are interested in salvation?

These "laws" that we have made up, that we project and pursue, are all based on fear, a sense of lack, insecurity, and so on. And because thought is external, they are maintained with images.

Are we beginning to see that if salvation is not one's whole function and purpose — a genuine goal — we just make ideas? We want to make ideas of truth. But we deceive only ourselves. The lesson continues:

> *While you would seek for it in things that have*
> *no meaning, you bind yourself to laws that*
> *make no sense.*

Unless we see that whatever we make has no sense, we will not be able to outgrow it. However, we do not want to outgrow anything. We just want to add more. Our goal is not to undo, but to "improve" by adding more. That is one of the misperceptions we all hold.

> *Thus do you seek to prove salvation is where it*
> *is not.*

We think salvation is in having more property, more money, more cars, more this and that, and so forth. We believe they would solve our problems. The

Course does not admit a problem is real. Mr. Krishnamurti said, "There are no problems apart from the mind." He would say, "Prove to me that problems are real." If we could prove to ourselves whether the problem is real or not, would we need anybody as a teacher? We would then become our own teacher and our own pupil.

But we stop short in our questioning. We just assume our problems are real.

> *Today we will be glad you cannot prove it. For if you could, you would forever seek salvation where it is not, and never find it. The idea for today tells you once again how simple is salvation.*

How simple is salvation! And we think it is so difficult.

> *Look for it where it waits for you, and there it will be found. Look nowhere else...*

Now who is going to stop, and look nowhere else? What would it take — what guts, what conviction, what integrity, what self-honesty — would it take not to look elsewhere? Is that our intent?

We do not know how to read the lesson. And, as a rule, we are not going to bring anything to application. All of our learning, explaining, and verbal understanding is an indulgence. Mr. Krishnamurti called it "entertainment." The brain only knows to seek entertainment.

> *Look nowhere else, for it is nowhere else.*

Can we honestly say that? If we can, we can also say, "I am under no laws but God's." But if we are looking for solutions and panaceas elsewhere, it is not true. Other than in the laws of God, salvation is nowhere. That is the decision one makes not to be swayed.

Most people have never made a decision from the day they were born. We have all chosen things — this versus that — depending on which is more important or more advantageous to us. Everyone is in the service of his own success and gain. But decision has nothing to do with any misperception. It knows, *I am under no laws but God's.*

And can anything intrude upon that knowing? That is a real knowing. One realizes the truth of it because one puts energy into it. First you *understand,* then you *realize,* and finally you *recognize* the truth and you are totally liberated. The Course calls it "simple." Yet try to see how simple it is.

> *Think of the freedom in the recognition that you are not bound by all the strange and twisted laws you have set up to save you.*

Now the lesson uses the word "recognition." We have gone from understanding to realizing in the first paragraph. And now, in the third paragraph, we have come to recognition. Would anybody notice that, why the Course uses "recognition" here? Do we want to recognize that we are not bound by all the strange and twisted laws we have set up to save ourselves?

That would reverse everything we think. What then prevents one from reversing? Is it not our inability and unwillingness to question? Our minds tell us that we are trapped in the world. But we like being trapped. Reversing the process is not really one's own need, is it?

> *You really think you would starve unless you have stacks of green paper strips and piles of metal discs.*

Isn't that something? Are we ever going to give that up? If we do not, we will never recognize.

> *You really think a small round pellet or some fluid pushed into your veins through a sharpened needle will ward off disease and death. You really think you are alone unless another body is with you.*

We have to look at these insane beliefs. We would agree with the Course, but that doesn't mean anything either. If we disagree, that doesn't mean anything either. There is no honesty in what we say because there is no honesty in the relative thought system. Anything we say is meaningless. Once one begins to recognize that, it is difficult to stay in thought.

It requires a conscious effort to step out of thought. Just seeing, just being aware, would have its own action. Why does the Course say salvation is so simple? Why? Because awareness makes no effort at all — it just sees the false as the false.

Now, are we going to make this an idea, that aware-ness has no effort in it, that it only sees the false as the false and undoes it? Are we now going to make this truth into an abstract idea?

It is insanity that thinks these things.

Can there be a stronger word, *It is* insanity *that thinks these things* ? What are we going to do with the challenge of seeing that we are insane? But we would not even read it. Are we going to accept the fact that, yes, we are preoccupied with insanity, always busy like an insect with our thoughts? If we said that, it would be an idea.

However, if we actually observe that we are constantly busy, then this observation is awareness. But awareness is not self-analysis. In awareness there is recognition; a person sees the truth. Whether we are with a teacher or we do it alone, the issue would still be that we have to see the fact as a fact. At best, most of us will see the idea and agree. But seeing the idea is not seeing a fact.

> *It is insanity that thinks these things. You call them laws, and put them under different names in a long catalogue of rituals that have no use and serve no purpose. You think you must obey the "laws" of medicine, of economics and of health.*[10]

More or less, all of the problems in the world today — whether national or individual — are problems of economy. The conflict of man against man or nation against nation, is all in the name of economy. All over the world, man is made more and more subject to the laws of economy. As long as economy is the law we obey, how controlled the individual is, and the nation remains subject to violence. It is even made profitable by the military industrial complex. Never in the history of man has violence been so commercialized.

We can observe the fact that, *The blind become accustomed to their world by their adjustment to it.*[11] And then it follows that, *Every adjustment is... a distortion, and calls upon defenses to uphold it against reality.*[12]

There is absolutely no humanism left in the world. Politics, government, and economy are all based on the continuation of tension, jealousy, and fear. So why would the Course not say that it is an insane way of thinking?

It is insanity that thinks these things.

We forget that. What would happen if we recognized, my God, that is insanity? We would see that *we* are part of insanity. If we saw it we would be finished with the world. Now what is the responsibility? Are we going to live insane lives? What are we going to do about our insanity? Whatever we do will either enhance insanity, or it will undo insanity. Are we going to enhance insanity, or are we going to dissolve it?

So, from this one begins to know who one is. We can see that we are not students and that we are not interested in undoing. Therefore, miracles have no meaning for us. We are not interested in the holy instant, and we do not care about the Holy Spirit because we are enhancing insanity. And yet the miracle, the holy instant, and the Holy Spirit, are there to help one undo insanity. Out of arrogance, we deny it. That is the nature of the ego.

> *These are not laws, but madness. The body is endangered by the mind that hurts itself. The body suffers just in order that the mind will fail to see it is the victim of itself. The body's suffering is a mask the mind holds up to hide what really suffers. It would not understand it is its own enemy; that it attacks itself and wants to die. It is from this your "laws" would save the body. It is for this you think you are a body.*

> *There are no laws except the laws of God. This needs repeating, over and over, until you realize it applies to everything that you have made in opposition to God's Will.*

God's Will is a fact. And for us to be extensions of God's Will there is no effort required — because it is God's Will we are extending. But we have set up our own will in place of His. And in that will there is no salvation, no peace, and no love; there is insecurity, insanity, and fear. Can we begin to see what the lesson means about insanity?

> *Your magic has no meaning. What it is meant to save does not exist. Only what it is meant to hide will save you.*

> *The laws of God can never be replaced. We will devote today to rejoicing that this is so.*

Well, who is going to rejoice? In order to rejoice, you have to change your whole mind.

> *It is no longer a truth that we would hide. We realize instead it is a truth that keeps us free forever.*

To be truthful is our own nature. Is there any struggle in it? To be false, there is struggle. Is there struggle in being honest? But we have reversed the process. Being honest is just about impossible. It has become the most difficult thing. Yet to be false and miserable has become natural.

The mind prefers to struggle and it hurts the body. That is the insanity of it. The wise person would never trust that. Just having read this one lesson — *I am under no laws but God's* — a person could be liberated. But most of us would want to put it into a nutshell, make it abstract, and know it as an idea.

> *Magic imprisons, but the laws of God make free. The light has come because there are no laws but His.*

Could one take on, that there are no other laws but His? Then we would say, "What am I going to do with myself?" We are afraid that we would sit around and rot. We need preoccupation. And preoccupation is born out of our fear of loneliness. We are so afraid to be alone! That is what the lesson said: you think you are going to be alone. Is there loneliness in wholeness?

There was a man in India who spent his life meditating and chanting the Vedas and other scriptures. And everybody liked him. He was meditating on being a holy man. Somehow life would have it that he came to see Mr. Krishnamurti. He sat down right away, chanting glorious mantras and showing Mr. Krishnamurti how holy he was. And Mr. Krishnamurti asked him, "What do you do all of this for?" "The name of God," was the man's reply. Mr. Krishnamurti said, "Forget your name of God."

The man did not know what to do. Finally he said to Mr. Krishnamurti, "But I do no harm! I'm not doing harm to anybody." Mr. Krishnamurti said, "That's something!" Which means that for us to be non-harmful — is just about impossible. We do not see that the man is doing harm. But in reality he is — he is harming himself.

We are all harmful as part of insanity extending insanity. Insanity is not something inactive; it is not dormant. We are responsible for the harm we bring to ourselves and to others by being part of the insanity. It is called being irresponsible. And we are dangerous. We cannot be friends, we cannot be honest, nor can we be loving. We have to see that we too are like the so-called holy man, saying, "I don't want to be disturbed. I want holiness."

We are frightened, but where does the fear come from? We are frightened to be honest. We are frightened to be sane, for we think we then would be alone. The fact is, fear is something by which we live. And we have found it useful because it keeps us preoccupied. So we put more alarms and locks on the doors and buy more insurance.

We will begin the longer practice periods today with a short review of the different kinds of "laws" we have believed we must obey.

Do we see that it says, "different kinds of laws"? But there are no different kinds of laws. There is only one Law, the Law of Love.

These would include, for example, the "laws" of nutrition, of immunization, of medication, and of the body's protection in innumerable ways. Think further; you believe in the "laws" of friendship, of "good" relationships and reciprocity. Perhaps you even think that there are laws which set forth what is God's and what is yours. Many "religions" have been based on this. They would not save but damn in Heaven's name. Yet they are no more strange than other "laws" you hold must be obeyed to make you safe.

There are no laws but God's. Dismiss all foolish magical beliefs today, and hold your mind in silent readiness to hear the Voice That speaks the truth to you.

This is "Voice" with a capital "V." But we are so preoccupied with our own chatter, that there is no space, not even a split second, for the other Voice to be heard. This Voice is always resounding within the mind. How preoccupied we must be not to hear It!

You will be listening to One Who says…

Would anybody notice the capital "W" on Who and know right away that this would be the absolute? We just read it, don't we? We will not even notice that One has a capital "O."

That Voice is within you. It is the Voice that is absolute. Yet we do not want to hear it and so It is left outside.

When we would not heed it *within*, the Teachers of God come to say it from outside so our physical ears may hear. That is why teachers are being prepared by the Course. Because one is asleep, maybe a brother could come from the outside and try to awaken him. He would say, "Look at this."

Such a teacher, who is extending sanity, would never commercialize. For love cannot be preached nor taught, it can only be shared. It is a joint venture, and a joyous adventure. No one can ever commercialize the absolute.

When the Course uses the words "One" and "Who," it means that it is the real Teacher who wants nothing.

You will be listening to One Who says…

And what does He say? Now one is really going to be very attentive. "My God. What is He going to say?" He says:

…there is no loss under the laws of God.

When the lesson says that He is going to speak to us, we would be grateful that He has spoken because it is most extraordinary, most peaceful. Our sleep would change, our diet would be different, everything is transformed.

One is totally transformed if one has heard it. Either we hear it from within or when the teacher comes, will we hear it then? If we still don't, something is wrong.

Payment is neither given nor received.

Isn't that beautiful? So then one would not go to people who want money or somebody else who is preaching or just pretending to be a teacher. It cannot be taught. The one whose words are true does not commercialize.

Exchange cannot be made; there are no substitutes; and nothing is replaced by something else. God's laws forever give and never take.

Wisdom always has something to give. But one wonders if anyone has the capacity to receive. What wisdom has to give is of the Kingdom of God. And wisdom never commercializes. Just as there are teachers, there is the inner Voice within you, too. It depends solely on the capacity to receive.

Hear Him Who tells you this...

Now is that going to make any difference? Are we going to hear Him? Did we hear Jesus, Sri Ramakrishna, or Mr. Krishnamurti?

Hear Him Who tells you this, and realize how foolish are the "laws" you thought upheld the world you thought you saw. Then listen further. He will tell you more. About the Love your Father has for you. About the endless joy He offers you.

It is so beautiful. The Course begins with undoing and telling us what we are not. Then it tells us who we are. But does it make any difference to us? We can read, *I am the light of the world,*[13] or *My holiness blesses the world,*[14] or *My mind is part of God's. I am very holy.*[15] They are immediately made into ideas.

Hear Him Who tells you this, and realize how foolish are the "laws" you thought upheld the world you thought you saw.

You thought you saw... means that you never did see.

Then listen further. He will tell you more. About the Love your Father has for you. About the endless joy He offers you. About His yearning for His only Son, created as His channel for creation; denied to Him by his belief in hell.

Let us today open God's channels to Him, and let His Will extend through us to Him.

This means that in wholeness there is the sharing of love. As love is shared, it intensifies its vitality. Wholeness gives to wholeness.

We can see how in nature the rains come, the rivers flow to the ocean, and millions of tons of water float up to the clouds; it rains bringing green vegetation, the water then goes into the rivers, and it goes on. This is the Action of Love. The perfection of it inspires one; it sustains life. It purifies the air we breathe and the things we eat. Can we see the miracle of it?

> Let us today open God's channels to Him, and let His Will extend through us to Him.

Would you have known that? That as I receive, I give, back and forth?

> Thus is creation endlessly increased. His Voice will speak of this to us, as well as of the joys of Heaven which His laws keep limitless forever. We will repeat today's idea until we have listened and understood there are no laws but God's. Then we will tell ourselves, as a dedication with which the practice period concludes:
>
> I am under no laws but God's.
>
> We will repeat this dedication as often as possible today; at least four or five times an hour, as well as in response to any temptation to experience ourselves as subject to other laws throughout the day. It is our statement of freedom from all danger and all tyranny. It is our acknowledgment that God is our Father, and that His Son is saved.[16]

By the time we have come to the last sentence, we have realized the truth. Thus, reading the lesson, starting with, *I am under no laws but God's,* and then reading the first and second page, we have evolved and been awakened. We have received the potentials of these holy words of the Course. As we come to the last sentence, we have: ...*our acknowledgement that God is our Father, and that His Son is saved.*

If you are under no laws but God's, you are His Holy Son. If you haven't heard it, then you are still outside. Which self do you want to identify with? Which one do you want to recognize as the truth?

There are no fears. *Nothing real can be threatened.* Only the Self — the Son of God, the God-created Self — is real. The one whom God created cannot be threatened. For:

> *Nothing real can be threatened.*
> *Nothing unreal exists.*

There are those who think that they are separated. But in God's Mind it is not so. In truth, it is not so. They are temporarily asleep.

Once the correction has been made internally, you see with different eyes. Your values change. You are not going to believe in the needles, the pellets, and the greenbacks. When your values have changed, you have already seen it.

There has to be the space where there is not the thought. But can you listen without the interruptions of thought? If you cannot, you are not listening, because you are interpreting. When you keep on interpreting, it means that you are preoccupied with thought.

Either you have heard what the Course has said or, when you do not hear it, you interpret it.

Then our likes and dislikes come in and we have made no contact with the lesson. And since we have no real contact with the lesson, when it tells us to repeat this four or five times an hour, we say, "Listen, I have more important things to do." We will not be able to find the time. How long will it take to repeat it — 30 seconds? So all told, in an hour, one could probably repeat it in two minutes.

Supposing you are awake sixteen hours — that would be 32 minutes of practicing. Yet we do not have the time because we are so preoccupied. So our values have not changed. As long as our values have not changed, there will not be the space within.

We started with:

I am under no laws but God's.

In that there is no fear. But if we want to be free of fear, we must live by the laws of God. There is no reaction, guilt, or punishment in the laws of God. The *Text* of the Course says that,

No penalty is ever asked of God's Son except by himself and of himself.[17]

Divine Laws are never in contradiction to peace, or to the serenity of one's own holiness.

We see laws as something to which we must conform. All we know is conformity — no matter how heroic we are. We are bound hand and foot. Conformity is the law of personal life. We are trained from childhood. And conformity always has problems. So we have to conform, and we have problems. That is the burden under which we live.

Wisdom lies in making space so that there is less preoccupation, less conformity, and fewer problems. Wisdom does not acknowledge problems. Unless there are different values and a new order in one's life, there is not the space for inspiration and joy. There is not the space for the new to take place. For the new to take place, one must make room.

The shedding away of what is meaningless is man's love for God. We must not be controlled externally. What we do, what we eat, when we go to bed — everything needs order and sanity. So the first step in coming to, *There is nothing to fear,*[18] is that you are not afraid to let go of the things of fear, of self-improvement, and all that is meaningless.

It is a kind of growing up. You are evolving and getting stronger. "Stronger" means you have more space to be:

I am as God created me.[19]

And then you can really say, *Nothing real can be threatened,* because you have actually experienced it. Now you see what is unreal. You are shedding the unessentials and therefore, making the space for the real. It is an inner transformation. It is effortless. It is very simple, and very basic to the Course.

We, as human beings, must radically and internally change in order to live by, *I am under no laws but God's.* A prayer in the *Text* reads,

Forgive us our illusions, Father, and help us to accept our true relationship with You, in which there are no illusions, and where none can ever enter.[20]

This requires a deep and radical change within the self. But where laziness and routine is a convenience, self-imposed helplessness will continue, along with its violence.

Laws are not political or economic, they are of God. In truth, you are the child of God. You are the light of peace upon the earth when your life is consistent with the peace of God that knows no other laws but love. We have to realize the obvious danger of allowing the manmade rules of time to interfere with the timeless Laws of Creation.

How glorious is the Course that offers the Son the absolute Thoughts of God. His Thought knows no conflict, no deprivation, no fear, no scarcity, and hence, no insecurity.

I am under no laws but God's.

This is a state of being that knows no fear, no insecurity, no violence, and no conformity to the rules of time.

You have all the help you need to bring *A Course In Miracles* into application. The guidance is ever there; in fact, you need not even seek it. You need only not ignore it. Be receptive to what is ever given. You will realize out of your gratefulness the Action of Grace that forever surrounds you with its blessing. To live by, *I am under no laws but God's,* all that is required is your willingness to heed.

Joining the Atonement is the way out of fear.[21]

The Holy Spirit brings one to one's own vast holiness, to the undivided wholeness of the Sonship.

"THE DREAM OF FEAR"

An excerpt* from
The Gifts Of God
by Helen Schucman

FEAR IS THE ONE EMOTION of the world. Its forms are many — call them what you will — but it is one in content. Never far, even in form, from what its purpose is, never with power to escape its cause, and never but a counterfeit of joy, it rests uncertainly upon a bed of lies. Here it was born and sheltered by its seeming comfort. Here it will remain where it was born, and where its end will come. For here is nothingness, where neither birth nor death is real, nor any form in the misshapen mind that spawned its seeming life has any meaning in the Mind of God.

If you were certain — wholly sure and with consistent grasp of what the world can give — fear would be laid aside as easily as joy and peace unite on love's

---

* "The Dream Of Fear" is the first section of five in the long blank verse poem entitled, "The Gifts Of God." It is printed here in prose form. This poem was written by Helen Schucman between February and April, 1978, some five years after *A Course In Miracles* was completed. See *The Gifts Of God* (Foundation for Inner Peace, 1982), pages 115-118. (Editor)

behalf. But first there must be certainty that there can be no love where fear exists, and that the world will never give a gift which is not made of fear, concealed perhaps, but which is surely present somewhere in the gift. Accept it not, and you will understand a gift far greater has been given you.

Let not the world deceive you. It was made to be deception. Yet its snares can be so easily escaped a little child can walk through safely, and without a care that would arrest its progress. Dreams are dreams, and every one is equally untrue. This is the only lesson to be learned. Yet will fear linger until every one is recognized as nothingness, and seen exactly as it is and nothing more. There is no person, thing or circumstance that you can value as your own without the "gift" of fear arising in your heart. For you have seen them all as they are not, and love for them has fled as if from you. And you will think that God has ceased to care for you who have betrayed the Son He loves, and chosen fear and guilt in place of Him.

Does God deceive or does the world? For it is sure that one must lie. There is no point at which their thoughts agree, their gifts unite in kind or purpose. What you take from one the other will obscure. There is no hope of compromise in this. Nor can there be a shifting of the mind between the two without the fear that every dream must bring. How fearful it must be to see yourself a maker of reality and truth, the lord of destiny and time's domain, and arbiter appointed for the world.

Dreams never change. Remember only this, but do not let it slip away at times and let yourself give way to fear again. Deny the dream but do not fail the truth, for only what is true will never fail. All else deceives. All else will terrify, and even when it seems to please the most it brings with it a heavy cost of pain. Be free of suffering now. There is no cost for any gift that comes to you from God. His way is certain, for His gifts remain forever as He gave them. Do not think that fear can enter where His gifts abide. But do not think gifts can be received where fear has entered, and has touched your sight with gross distortions that the world thinks real.

There are no scraps of dreams. Each one contains the whole of fear, the opposite of love, the hell that hides the memory of God, the crucifixion of His holy Son. Therefore, be vigilant against them all, for in their single purpose they are one, and hell is total. It can seem to take forever for this lesson to be learned, and yet it need not be. I come to speak in time of timelessness. Have you not learned the pain of dreaming yet? There is no need to hug it to your heart, and to forget the dreadful cost of salvaging despair and building up deceptions once again.

The tiniest of dreams, the smallest wish for values of the world is large enough to stand between you and the sweet release that God would offer you. He cannot choose to change His Son, nor make your mind accept the perfect freedom He has given you. Yet it is certain you will turn to Him and suddenly remember. But be sure of this and do not let it slip away: What God has joined is one. And one as well is everything that fear has made to be the great deceiver and the substitute for God's creation. You can choose but one, and which you choose is total. Everything the world can offer promises some joy that it will never give. And everything that God has promised you will never fail in anything. No need will be unmet, no hurt unhealed, no sorrow kept unchanged, no darkness undispelled. The smallest pain will vanish suddenly before His gifts. An unremembered world will leave no trace behind its going, when God's gifts have been accepted as the only things you want.

"Choose once again" is still your only hope. Darkness cannot conceal the gifts of God unless you want it so. In peace I come, and urge you now to make an end to time and step into eternity with me. There will not be a change that eyes can see, nor will you disappear from things of time. But you will hold my hand as you return because we come together. Now the hosts of Heaven come with us, to sweep away all vestiges of dreams and every thought that rests on nothingness. How dear are you to God, Who asks but that you walk with me and bring His light into a sickened world which fear has drained of love and life and hope.

Surely you will not fail to hear my call, for I have never failed to hear your cries of pain and grief, and I have come to save and to redeem the world at last from fear. It never was, nor is, nor yet will be what you imagine. Let me see for you, and judge for you what you would look upon. When you have seen with me but once, you would no longer value any fearful thing at cost of glory and the peace of God.

This is my offering: A quiet world, with gentle ordering and kindly thought, alive with hope and radiant in joy, without the smallest bitterness of fear upon its loveliness. Accept this now, for I have waited long to give this gift to you. I offer it in place of fear and all the "gifts" that fear has given you. Can you choose otherwise, when all the world is standing breathless, waiting on your choice? Come now to me and we will go to God. There is no way that we can go alone. But when we come together there can be no way in which the World of God can fail. For His the Word that makes us one in Him, and mine the Voice that speaks this Word to you.

ADDENDA

AUTOBIOGRAPHY
OF TARA SINGH

TARA SINGH, founder of the Foundation for Life
Action and the teacher of the School at *The Branching
of the Road*[1] spent his early years in a village in Punjab,
India.

"I came from a background in India of
living in a spacious house with one door,
where my parents and grandparents,
sisters, uncles, aunts, cousins, and nephews
lived together. The one door signifies that
our house was not divided and for centuries
we had lived in harmony. Wisdom resided
there and lifted us out of irritation and
reaction. The elders extended goodness and
we grew up surrounded with affection and
a sense of reverence for life. No one in the
family had ever been career oriented. We
had agricultural land and were an honored
family. We considered ourselves affluent.
The one door stood as the symbol of unity.

"The family was religious and even without knowing it, I absorbed the values of the spirit. Some of us extended ourselves beyond the village and beyond the boundaries of self-centeredness.

"During my formative years, there was an innate resistance to imposed, formal education. I sensed that it was not right and felt false submitting to it. It was so much inferior to what one learned directly. *That* I enjoyed and the imposed appeared harmful. The teacher even had to resort to tying me to a tree during the sixth months that I attended school because I repeatedly ran away to play in the fields or by the village pond. All my life, however, I learned through what awakened my interest. And I later discovered that natural intelligence is autonomous; it can cope with anything and has its own capacity to learn."

From this sheltered environment, at the age of nine, Tara Singh and his mother and uncles traveled to Panama via Europe to join his father who was in business there. While in Panama he attended school for two years. At the age of eighteen, he and his mother returned to India and he found himself caught in a conspiracy to get him married. Inspired by the family saint, at the age of twenty-one, his search for truth and God led him to the Himalayas.

"For four years I wholeheartedly applied myself to a religious life of devotion and discipline. I had flashes of insight that led me to question and to undo my own knowing. I realized that truth is independent of time and conventional religion, and a mind conditioned by religious or secular beliefs is always limited. I emerged from the solitary years with discrimination and the capacity to receive and to heed. Disillusionment brought about a sudden change of value, but to be freed from the mask of pious attitude and to outgrow tradition is an invaluable experience. Now I insisted upon being responsible, on questioning and coming to clarity before getting involved."

In his next phase of growth, Tara Singh responded to the poverty of India through participation in that country's postwar industrialization. The great beings he met were his best teachers. He was forever affected by how wisely they lived and the goodness they shared.

"There were several wise men of intrinsic life and consistent knowledge who made a strong impact on my life. One of the most extraordinary men was Giani Kartar Singh. I met him on a train at Amritsar on the way to Lahore in 1945. He came and sat opposite me in the compartment. I was in crisis, burning to make contact and not knowing how to approach him. But the energy of first thought acts involuntarily. Gianiji, an eminent man, was the saintly, genius leader of the Sikhs. His Sikhism encompassed all humanity in its range; his nationalism was unlimited humanism.

"This contact opened totally new dimensions and potentials within me and made things possible in an India besieged by the cruelty of poverty. It culminated in an enormous industrial project at the grass roots level with capital of over six million dollars, supported by Sikhs, Maharajahs, and others, but most of all by Gianiji's impeccable integrity.

"He was a man of renunciation and religious outlook who never had a bank account. The force of his love transformed my life and in his atmosphere, I blossomed. He offered an intimate relationship through which I became a friend of Prime Minister Nehru and other eminent leaders of incorruptible lives. He had said when people asked him, 'What do you see in Tara Singh?'

'The word "impossible" does not apply to him. He will not accept second best and this will make him or break him.'

"In 1947, the advent of freedom and the partition of India and Pakistan disrupted the humanistic plan. I was virtually penniless and homeless but felt the need to visit the West and make an individual survey of the impact of science on society before embarking upon another venture. One questioned what part the gigantic, underdeveloped, agrarian society of almost two billion was to play in the Post War period. Would the west heed India's authentic voice — the wisdom of its unbiased outlook — and avert the spread of tension? The media was accelerating Cold War propaganda, and nationalism was being drummed into the collective consciousness."

It was in the 1950's, discovering that man's problems cannot be solved externally, that Mr. Singh was inspired by his association with Mr. J. Krishnamurti.

"At the end of 1947, soon after the independence of India, I arrived in England and then came to New York to meet with those at an international level who made decisions and determined human destiny. In the West, I met a great many men and women of excellence. Very quickly I came into contact with the mind of the age and found there was little use for wisdom which never makes survival its first concern. Skills had become important and man was rapidly losing his work and becoming subject to jobs. I was startled by the power of the media with its ability to influence collective consciousness, the panic about communism, and the stimulated daily life obsessed with problems. These were just facts, not good or bad, but what was.

"The background of the Sikh religion prior to meeting Gianiji was essential to the new awakening. Similarly, before meeting with Mr. J. Krishnamurti, it was essential to be aware of world affairs. For me the cultural life of New York City revolved around the work of the United Nations and various philanthropic organizations. I was captivated by the creative spirit of the West. New York at the time seemed like the capital of the world and I was overwhelmed by the music, art, theatre, and literature which it offered. Also, contact with the lofty voices of the forefathers of the New World — Emerson, Thoreau, Whitman, and Lincoln — enriched my life.

"It was in New York that I literally learned to read. Loneliness compelled me to it. Usually the hours spent reading from 8:00 p.m. to 2:00 a.m. became the most rewarding time in my life and this continued for years irrespective of where I lived in the world.

"To outgrow is always blessed — not to get stuck, but to be enriched by the deeper expression of life on the planet. It was a good background to meet with Mr. Krishnamurti and enter the realm of Eternal Laws.

"It was on my second trip to America, in 1953, that I met Mr. Krishnamurti in New

York. In twenty minutes, all that I knew or pretended to know, or wished to do, disappeared. The contact was so strong it put an end to the bondage of my knowing and lifted me to what is not of words. Never could I have conceived the blessing of such a sacred encounter. I remember thinking to myself as I walked through Central Park that it was a blessing to be born at the time that such a great being was upon the planet. The unchangeable light of his word extended itself and still continues to expand its newness in me.

"A few years later, I arrived in Ojai, California, a week before the annual 'Talks' began and met with Mr. Krishnamurti daily. When I attended his first 'Talk' at the end of that week, he looked at everyone in the audience prior to beginning to speak, as was his custom. When his eyes met mine for a fleeting instant, it imparted a joy, a tremendous blessing, and I was given 'the ears to hear.' After the 'Talk' I sat for hours transfixed.

"The next day, when I met with him, I told him that I understood what he had shared beyond the words. We sat in silence a while and then he said:

> 'Drop everything.
> Be still.
> The seeds are sown, leave it alone.'

"It took years for me to know the full significance of his words. Year after year, I continued to discover what 'the seeds are sown' meant and the responsibility that Mr. Krishnamurti assumed. The God-lit Teacher imparts the energy that brings one to stillness and the gratefulness out of which the next action emerges. He guarded me directly, and indirectly, from ever getting involved in what was not part of creation — *the carnival* in the end to extend the True Knowledge of eternal seeds with which he blessed me. The energy of gratefulness then enabled me to relate with what is eternal.

"The only true relationship is between the Teacher and the student. It is not between parents and children, nor between wives and husbands. All these fall short of timelessness. It is the relationship with the Teacher that ends the separation and brings one to the Oneness of Life and the One Mind of God. The relationship is eternal and does not end in death. Its action continues as the student harnesses the energy of joyous responsibility and realizes that which is real emerges out of his own stillness and gratefulness. From 1953, meetings with Mr. Krishnamurti continued now and then. I was not a regular devotee, but he remained my constant companion in life.

"In 1963, I brought all loose ends to a head and had even outgrown wanting to help the world. I had been involved in world affairs, increasing the per capita income of underdeveloped areas. Through this work I realized:

> Times will reveal themselves — that you cannot depend on the externals. Without the externals, there is no personality and there is no relationship at the personality level. The fear of the externals will destroy the manmade, external world.

"I felt the spaciousness of noninvolvement with either person, place, or activity and went to Switzerland to attend Mr. Krishnamurti's 'Talks.' Early in 1964, I had an interview with him in Madras. I said that I had come to give myself totally to a life of the spirit. He startled me by saying: 'Go and earn some money.' But I said, 'Sir, I have made up my mind. I do not want to live the life of the world. It has no fascination for me.' He stopped me short and repeated what he had said before, 'Go and earn some money.'

"I was under the impression that a sannyasi who lived a vertical life did not touch money. The tradition in India was established that men and women of renunciation were fed by the householder. I pleaded my seriousness. Mr. Krishnamurti said, 'Go and earn some money or I will never see you again.' This time, the *or else* gave me no option but to heed. Instantly the duality ended and my own heeding transmitted a sense of joy so energetic its profound meaning still continues to unfold.

> His words, when heeded, are those
> that have no ending.
> They light the passage of your life.

"I had only about $20 in all to my name when I started. As I was leaving, an additional instruction was given by Mr. Krishnamurti: 'Do not ever take advantage of another.'

"How difficult it is to end the preference for advantages. One wants to lead a spiritual life, but could this ever be within our present thought system based on motives?

"The words of Mr. Krishnamurti, who was free of personality, and like Jesus and Lord Buddha owned nothing, ordain an action in one that contains the vitality to actualize its completion. This discovery is the blessing. I learned that the Action of Life is impersonal; activity is devoid of action. My whole mind gathered itself to earning money and within four months I had acquired sixty thousand dollars.

"In this age, it is difficult to lead a truly religious life without one's own independent means. Without money, one invariably resorts to exploitation and ends up needing people for one's own projects.

"The responsibility for the right use of money was the next step. What wisdom it would take to make right use of a dollar.

I will not value what is valueless.[2]

"What discrimination it takes to end wastage, deny yourself nothing, nor look at price tags, but be with the essential always."

Subsequently, Tara Singh became more and more removed from worldly affairs and devoted several years of his life to the study and the practice of Raja Yoga and the non-commercial lifestyle of the enlightened beings of the Vedas and the Upanishads. During this time he also came into close contact with the teachings of Sri Ramakrishna and Sri Ramana Maharshi. The discipline imparted through Raja Yoga helped make possible a three year period of silent retreat.

"Mr. Krishnamurti warned me that Hatha Yoga is merely physical, and stressed the importance of health and discipline in life. The deeper meaning of discipline that is not imposed but has its own order began to reveal itself. It awakened a passion that had no alternatives. This led me to spend three years in silence in Carmel, California.

"Silence, ever whole, has its own wisdom of non-dependence and succeeds effortlessly in coping with all the essentials without the need of another. It has its own independent existence. Not imposed from without, it is of an inner yearning to be with the spacious aloneness in which one is related to all that is. Silence is <u>not</u> isolation seeking some projected goal of self-improvement.*

"As I emerged from silence, I saw that hardly anyone listens and realized why Jesus placed so much emphasis on having 'the ears to hear.' Without it, one cannot communicate. Learning is abstract; it is of things and ideas that have names; it is deceptive for it is based on interpretation. But to communicate and to heed demands an attentive, receptive, and silent mind. Self-honesty or truth requires consistency at all levels of one's being.

"Inwardly, there arose a <u>yearning in me to be productive.</u> True productivity is not projected but is independent of the externals. It is <u>without direction.</u> It can only be the extension of the Divine Will, the only Reality."

---

* For more discussion on silence as a state of being, see "Silence" in Tara Singh's *The Voice That Precedes Thought* (Foundation for Life Action, 1987), pages 89-103. (Editor)

As he emerged from the years of silence in 1976, he came into contact with *A Course In Miracles*. Its impact on him was profound. He recognized its unique contribution as a scripture and saw it as the answer to man's urgent need for direct contact with True Knowledge. The Course has been the focal point of his life ever since.

"When I discovered *A Course In Miracles* and read in the Introduction:

> *Nothing real can be threatened.*
> *Nothing unreal exists.*

I recognized the power of the Word of God in it and also, for the first time, my function in life. A direct relationship with the scribe came into being for which I will be forever grateful. One is grateful for what is timeless — forever the strength and light of your life. This benediction is your constant companion.

"You realize there is nothing to achieve, perfection is ever complete. God's Plan for Salvation is already accomplished.[3] The truth of this is what brings learning *almost to its appointed end*.[4]

"The wise, it is said, remains ever the stranger to doubt and despair."

The Foundation for Life Action, a federally approved, nonprofit, educational foundation, begun in 1980 on the principles of rightness, virtue, and having something to give, started with no money and the conviction not to seek or live off donations. It came to self-reliance by doing workshops and retreats throughout the country, sharing mostly the principles of *A Course In Miracles*, providing an atmosphere of friendship and one-to-one relationship. In 1981, Tara Singh realized that in order to bring the Course into application, something was required other than mere workshops and retreats. They had served their purpose.

Since Easter, 1983, Mr. Singh has conducted the Non-Commercialized Retreat: A Serious Study of *A Course In Miracles* — an unprecedented, in-depth exploration of the Course at no tuition charge.

> "At the height of prosperity, the decision was made to end workshops and retreats and to begin the non-commercialized action — probably the first time it has been offered in the New World. I was told that the Course is to be lived and spent a hundred days to discover intimately what is entailed in bringing it into application. I realized that the Name of God cannot be commercialized. It is something you receive while you give and fulfills the law that one must teach in order to learn. How can the energy of love be sold?"

Mr. Singh has chosen to work closely on a one-to-one basis with serious students. The program is sponsored by the Foundation for Life Action.

"For the past six years, *A Course In Miracles* has been shared non-commercially. It is a one-to-one, intimate atmosphere where the 'Given' is made accessible. But it is for those having the energy of the first thought. For us the student is one whose first love is God.

"The School at *The Branching of the Road* is in the spirit of the Upanishads and the wise men of ancient India and China — where the Teacher and the student lived together and wisdom was neither bought nor sold. The only requirement was a student with the capacity to receive. Self-honesty and the passion to know the truth of man, God, and creation were essential, as well as having no unwillingness that blocks and evades the holy instant.

Philosophers, educators, gurus —
the interpreters of knowledge —
and others who share their ideas and beliefs,
want to conform us to think in a certain way.

I do not fall into any of these categories.
For me, religious life
is not a concept or a dogma.
It is a state of being.

Absolute Knowledge cannot be interpreted.
It transcends learning.
We can be made aware
of the limitations of our conditioning
and can question our conclusions,

the fallacy of external authority,
as well as our faith in insecurity.

All of this is still in the realm of thought,
adjustments, and changes of attitude.
As long as there is relative knowledge
conflict remains our lot
and we are ever unfulfilled.

It is undoing by which man is awakened
from the illusion of learning
and the preoccupation
with accumulating information.
Undoing,
by which the awakening can take place,
is of your own energy,
your own internal clarity.

Teaching and learning
are not what the School
at *The Branching of the Road* is about.
The School is for those
who come not to *learn* but to *Be*.*
There is no authority.
It is consistent with
"where two or more gather in His Name"[5]
to jointly explore and undo past knowing.
The School is for those
who refuse to be influenced by another
and realize that only the newness

---

* Refers to the song, "The Seventy," sung at the first Forty Days in the Wilderness Retreat. See *The Voice That Precedes Thought* by Tara Singh (Foundation for Life Action, 1987), page 282. (Editor)

within man
can transform his life.

It takes great wisdom and integrity
to come to a silent mind,
to dispel the insanity of helplessness.,
True Knowledge is free of conflict
and acknowledges no problem as real.

I am not here to persuade the student
to think in a particular way,
or to give instructions,
or to conform anyone to any ideals.
The School is based on
dissolving misperception
and acknowledges no problem as real.
We do not direct the student
to follow a certain thought system
or a method of solving problems.

The student must be highly responsible
to be a participant
of the one-to-one relationship of the School
to realize the clarity
that frees one from dependence.

> *Forgive us our illusions, Father,*
> *and help us to accept*
> *our true relationship with You,*
> *in which there are no illusions,*
> *and where none can ever enter.*[6]

"What we share — impart — is self-reliance. To come to self-reliance is essential, especially at this time when the monetary system of the world is in control of the lives of men. Since man has lost his work, he has become subject to jobs. Now he must find his own inner calling and come to intrinsic work. The Foundation for Life Action provides a productive life of intrinsic work where one can come to self-reliance by having something to give to the world. We undertake to live by holy relationship to discover the Self that is not a body. To know:

I am sustained by the love of God.[7]

is our undertaking — to forgive and not to judge as a process of self learning. It is an internal action since wisdom begins with the knowledge of self."

Tara Singh offered the Forty Days In The Wilderness Retreat in Angel Fire, New Mexico, from April 10 through May 20, 1989. This retreat marked a turning point in his life and in the development of the Foundation for Life Action. The Joseph's Plan,[8] which the retreat initiated, is to meet the primary needs of man for food, shelter, clothing, and contact with the Spirit in times to come.*

Tara Singh is the author of numerous books and has been featured on many video and audio tapes in which he discusses the action of bringing one's life into order, freeing oneself from past conditioning,

---

* Please refer to the Introduction of *"Nothing Real Can Be Threatened,"* pages 24-27, for further discussion of Joseph's Plan. (Editor)

living the principles of *A Course In Miracles*, and coming to inner awakening.

His life is dedicated to:

"I will not be dishonest to myself."

and to the fact that the Name of God cannot be commercialized. His thought system is not of lack. He has no goals, therefore, no doubt.

"God's Plan for Salvation represents humanity. It is not a religion or an organization. Its purpose is to come to inner peace."

In answer to the question, "What kind of life do you envision for yourself?" Tara Singh responded:

"Rightness.

Rightness is independent of personality
and its consequences.
It stands vertical — a law unto itself.
Nothing of the body senses can affect
or obscure it.
Rightness is independent
of the limitations of right and wrong,
thus free of judgment and conflict,
free of lack, of seeking and trying,
free of thought, feelings, and reactions.

Such a man is liberated
from the illusion of time
and its beliefs and concepts.

Ever stable, stately and uninvolved,
he knows no loss, gain, or unfulfillment.

Such a man is an extension
of the grace of God.
He has an atmosphere of purity
surrounding him.
It is a blessing to be in his presence
and to have the ears to hear
his eternal Words."

For additional autobiographical material, see the Introduction of Tara Singh's *How To Raise A Child Of God* (Life Action Press, 1987), pages 11-42. (Editor)

The Purpose
Of The
Foundation For Life Action

The Purpose of the Foundation for Life Action
is to be with the Eternal Laws
so that it does not become an organization.

LOVE IS ETERNAL.
ABILITIES EXTENDING LOVE ARE BLESSED.

In the absence of Love
abilities become the bondage of skills,
limited to personality.
Among virtuous men,
it is what the human being is that is Real,
and not what he does in a body.

The Purpose of the Foundation is to be part of

GOD'S PLAN FOR SALVATION.[1]

Thus it has a different point of reference
than the thought system of man.

Obviously, the Name of God
cannot be commercialized.
There are no fees in what we share.
We do not believe in loss and gain.
Non-commercialized action is provided by
the blessings of productive life.

"In God We Trust"

Those who are with the Eternal Laws
in times of change remain unaffected.
In crisis, it is your care for another
that is your strength.

We have a function in the world
to be truly helpful to others,
knowing:

> *I am sustained by the Love of God.*[2]

> *My only function is the one God gave me.*[3]

> *Nothing real can be threatened.*
> *Nothing unreal exists.*

We are not pressured by the brutality of success.
We are blessed by the work we do.
Gratefulness is complete, as love is independent.

To us, the human being comes first.
Thus it enables us to go past
the conventional opinion of right and wrong
and relate directly to you.

For man is as God created him,
unchanged by the changeable society
that rules his body with its belief systems.

The Truth is a Fact that dissolves illusions of time.
Our function is to dispel the abstraction of ideas
and realize the actuality of Fact.

For,

> *I am under no laws but God's.*[4]

<u>Reverence for Life</u> is of a still mind
hallowed by His Love.
This transformation is what we call

THE PATH OF VIRTUE.

The Path of Virtue is the ministry of gratefulness.
The wise who extends
the Kingdom of God on earth
lives consistent with

"BUT SEEK YE FIRST
THE KINGDOM OF GOD,
AND HIS RIGHTEOUSNESS;
AND ALL THINGS
SHALL BE ADDED UNTO YOU."[5]

Statement Of The Participants
Of The
One Year Non-Commercialized Retreat

As students of *A Course In Miracles*,
we are the disciples of the One
in charge of Atonement.
He is to us — Alive.
We think with Him.
Whatever we do, is done by — Him.

Ours is the Ministry of Gratefulness.
Together, productive and self-reliant,
we stand on our own feet
to bring the Course into application in our lives and
to prepare to see man, in Truth,
as the Altar of God on Earth.
And to extend to the tired world,
taxed by meaningless work,
the message of — Fulfillment.

We have no projects,
no ambition to own a community,
or external ashrams.
We do not commercialize life,
nor ask for donations.

Our own sincerity and purity of work
makes our life intrinsic.
We are strengthened by the power
of seeing a — Fact,

and the integrity of single purpose.
We do not work for another
and see no man contaminated by external unreality.

We have found our — Calling,
having heard the whisper of Absolute Knowledge.
Gratefulness, Forgiveness,
Non-attachment are — Real.
And fulfillment already is a part of — Love.

"IN GOD WE TRUST."

Our lesson for today is:

*My mind is part of God's.
I am very holy.*[10]

REFERENCES

References are cited for the first edition of *A Course in Miracles*, ©1975, followed in brackets by the corresponding book, chapter, section, paragraph, sentence, and page for the second edition, ©1992, of the *Course*. For example, [T-16. III. 4;1. page 335.] refers to Text, Chapter 16, Section III, paragraph 4, sentence 1, page 335.

INTRODUCTION

1. *A Course in Miracles* (ACIM), first published in 1976 by the Foundation for Inner Peace, Glen Ellen, California, is a contemporary scripture that deals with the psychological/ spiritual issues facing humanity today. It consists of three volumes: *Text* (I) [T], *Workbook for Students* (II) [W], and *Manual for Teachers* (III) [M]. The *Text*, 622 pages (669 pages in second edition), sets forth the concepts on which the thought system of the *Course* is based. The *Workbook for Students*, 478 pages (488 pages in second edition), is designed to make possible the application of the concepts presented in the *Text* and consists of three hundred and sixty-five lessons, one for each day of the year. The *Manual for Teachers*, 88 pages (92 pages in second edition), provides answers to some of the basic questions a student of the

Course might ask and defines many of the terms used in the *Text*. (Editor)

2. *Nothing real can be threatened. Nothing unreal exists.* appears in the Introduction of *A Course In Miracles.* The complete introduction reads:

This is a course in miracles. It is a required course. Only the time you take it is voluntary. Free will does not mean that you can establish the curriculum. It means only that you can elect what you want to take at a given time. The course does not aim at teaching the meaning of love, for that is beyond what can be taught. It does aim, however, at removing the blocks to the awareness of love's presence, which is your natural inheritance. The opposite of love is fear, but what is all-encompassing can have no opposite.

This course can therefore be summed up very simply in this way:

> **Nothing real can be threatened.**
> **Nothing unreal exists.**
> *Herein lies the peace of God.*

3. ACIM, II, page 42. [W-27. 4;4-5. page 42.]
4. ACIM, I, page 6. [T-1. III. 1;1. page 8.]
5. ACIM, I, page 290. [T-15. V. 1;1-2. page 312.]
6. ACIM, I, page 337. [T-17. V. 1;1-7. page 362.]
7. See ACIM, I, page 354-356. [T-18. IV. pages 380-382.]
8. ACIM, II, page 32. [W-21. page 32.]
9. See Isaiah 6;9-10; Matthew 11:15 and 13:13-23.
10. *A Course In Miracles* refers to this principle many times, usually as *Seek and do not find.* See, for example: I, pages 208, 210, and 318: and II, page 120. [T-12. IV. 4;1-5. page 224.] [T-12. V. 7;1-2. page 226.] [T-16. V. 6;5. page 342.] [W-71. 4;1-2. page 121.]
11. These are the words spoken by Dr. William Thetford to Dr. Helen Schucman that initiated *A Course In Miracles.* See ACIM, Preface to the softcover edition, page 1. (Editor) [ACIM-Preface. page vii.]
12. ACIM, II, page 239. [W-133. page 245.]
13. Mr. J. Krishnamurti (1895-1986) was a world renowned teacher and philosopher. (Editor)

14. The Essenes were a religious sect of ascetics and mystics that existed from approximately the second century B.C. to the second century A.D. (Editor)

15. The benefit retreat, entitled the *The Awakening Of Intelligence*, was held in Santa Barbara, California, June 5-10, 1988. (Editor)

16. The *Mahabharata* is the famous Hindu epic which tells the "...tale of heroic men and women, some of whom were divine. It is a whole literature in itself, containing a code of life, a philosophy of social and ethical relations and speculative thought on human problems...He who knows it not, knows not the heights and depths of the soul..." From "Kulapati's Preface" to *Mahabharata* by C. Rajagopalachari (Bharatiya Vidya Bhavan, Bombay, 1951), page 2. (Editor)

17. ACIM, II, page 79. [W-50. page 79.]

18. ACIM, II, page 101. [W-61. 5;3-5. page 102.]

19. ACIM, II, page 374. [W-200. page 384.]

20. ACIM, II, page 447. [W-314. page 457.]

21. The one commandment given by Jesus, "Love ye one another," appears many times in the New Testament. See, for example: John 13:34-35, 15:12, 15:17; Romans 13:8.

22. Matthew 6:33.

23. Tara Singh's work with *A Course In Miracles* centers around his one-to-one relationship with a small number of serious students. This work is sponsored by the Foundation for Life Action, which is often called the School at *The Branching of the Road*. See ACIM, I, page 444, for clarification of the phrase, *The Branching of the Road*. For an account of what brought the School into being and what function it serves, see "The School – 'Having The Ears To Hear,'" in Tara Singh's *Dialogues On A Course In Miracles* (Life Action Press, 1987), pages 337-365. (Editor)

24. Refers to Joseph of the Old Testament. See Genesis 37 and following.

25. From the *Bhagavad Gita*, a portion of the Hindu epic, the *Mahabharata*. (Editor)

26. ACIM, II, page 191. [W-108. page 195.]

27. "In God We Trust" appears to have been inspired by a line from *The Star Spangled Banner*, "In God is our trust," written by Francis Scott Key in 1814. "In God We Trust" first appeared on the coinage of the United States in 1864, during the presidency of Abraham Lincoln. It became the official motto of the United States in 1956. (Editor)
28. Refers to Jesus' multiplying of fish and bread to feed the multitudes. See Matthew 14:15-21 and 15:32-38; Mark 6:35-44, and in the other two gospels of the New Testament. (Editor)

CHAPTER ONE
THERE ARE NO PROBLEMS APART FROM THE MIND

1. ACIM, III, page 1. [M-introduction. 2;2. page 1.]
2. ACIM, II, page 72. [W-45. 7;1-4. page 72.]
3. ACIM, I, page 208. See also: References, Introduction, no.10. [T-12. IV. 4;1-5. page 224.]
4. ACIM, II, page 33. [W-22. 1;1-6 and 2;1-5. page 33.]
5. ACIM, I, page 275. [T-14. XI. 1;1-9 and 2;1. page 296.]
6. ACIM, II, page 91. [W-56. 1;2-6. page 92.]
7. ACIM, II, page 79. [W-50. page 79.]
8. For clarification of the phrase, God's plan for salvation, see ACIM, I, pages 426-427;II, page 120 and following.(Editor) [T-21. V. 5;1-11 and 6;1-6. page 457.] Also [W-71. page 121.]
9. ACIM, II, page 189. [W-107. page 192.]
10. ACIM, I, page 39. [T-3. IV. 7;8-15. pages 43-44.]
11. ACIM, II, page 162. [W-94. page 164.]
12. ACIM, I, page 604. [T-31. II. 8;1-3. page 650.]
13. ACIM, II, page 332. [W-182. 8;1-3. page 340.]

CHAPTER TWO
"NOTHING REAL CAN BE THREATENED"

1. ACIM, II, page 315. [W-169. 1;3-4 and 3;4-6. page 323.]
2. ACIM, II, page 304. [W-164. 5;1-6. page 311.]
3. ACIM, III, page 62. [M-26. 4;8. page 65.]
4. ACIM, II, page 32. [W-21. page 32.]
5. ACIM, II, page 107. [W-65. page 108.]

6. ACIM, II, page 174. [W-99. page 177.]
7. ACIM, II, page 159. [W-93. page 161.]
8. ACIM, II, page 174. [W-99. page 177.]
9. ACIM, II, page 239. [W-133. page 245.]
10. ACIM, II, page 107. [W-65. page 108.]
11. ACIM, I, page 325. [T-16. VII. 6;4-6. page 349.]
12. ACIM, II, page 69. [W-44. page 69.]
13. *A Course in Miracles* defines a teacher of God as *...anyone who chooses to be one. His qualifications consist solely in this; somehow, somewhere he has made a deliberate choice in which he did not see his own interests as apart from someone else's.... Their function is to save time.... There is a course for every teacher of God. The form of the course varies greatly. So do the particular teaching aids involved. But the content of the course never changes. Its central theme is always, 'God's Son is guiltless, and in his innocence is his salvation.' It can be taught by actions or thoughts; in words or soundlessly; in any language or in no language; in any place or time or manner....* See ACIM, III, page 3. [M-1. 1;1-2 and 2;11 and 3;1-6. page 3.]

The *Course* also points out that the teacher of God *...cannot claim that title until he has gone through the workbook, since we are learning within the framework of our course.* See ACIM, III, page 38. [M-16. 3;7. page 40.]
14. ACIM, II, page 77. [W-48. page 77.]
15. ACIM, II, page 32. [W-21. page 32.]

CHAPTER THREE
FREEDOM FROM FEAR

1. John 13:34.
2. ACIM, I, page 179. [T-11. Introduction. 2;6. page 193.]
3. Ibid. [T-11. Introduction. 3;5-10. pages 193-194.]
4. ACIM, III, page 10. [M-4. II. 1;5-9. pages 11-12.]
5. ACIM, II, page 435. [W-293. page 445.]
6. See Plato's "Socrates' Defense (Apology)" at 21a, translated by Hugh Tredennick, in *The Collected Dialogues Of Plato* (Princeton University Press, 1961), page 7.
7. John 14:12.
8. Op. cit., at 17a, page 4.

9. See Plato's "Crito" at 46c, translated by Hugh Tredennick, in *The Collected Dialogues of Plato* (Princeton University Press, 1961), page 31.
10. See Plato's "Phaedo" at 84e, translated by Hugh Tredennick, in *The Collected Dialogues of Plato* (Princeton University Press, 1961), page 67.
11. ACIM, II, page 347. [W-188. 1;1-4 and 2;1-2 and 3;1-2. page 357.]

CHAPTER FOUR
LETTING GO IS THE ISSUE - DISCUSSIONS ON FEAR

1. ACIM, I, page 450. [T-22. VI. 13;10. page 483.]
2. ACIM, II, page 5. [W-3. page 5.]
3. ACIM, II, page 65. [W-42. page 65.]
4. ACIM, I, Introduction. [T-introduction. 1;8. page 1.]
5. ACIM, I, page 12. [T-1. VI. 5;7-8. page 14.]
6. ACIM, II, page 235. [W-131. 15;6. page 241.]
7. ACIM, I, page 326. The prayer in which this phrase appears has been referred to as *A Course In Miracles'* version of the Lord's Prayer. See: *Journey Without Distance: The Story Behind A Course In Miracles* by Robert Skutch (Celestial Arts, 1984), page 68. This prayer is discussed in great detail in *Dialogues On A Course In Miracles* by Tara Singh (Life Action Press, 1987), pages 35-167. (Editor) [T-16. VII. 12;1-7. page 350.]
8. ACIM, II, page 364. [W-196. page 374.]
9. From the Preface to the softcover edition of *A Course In Miracles*, [page 5.] This is a paraphrase of *Course* teachings. (Editor) [T-Preface. page xii.]
10. ACIM, II, page 119. [W-70. 9;3-4. page 120.]
11. ACIM, I, page 49. [T-4. I. 6;3. page 54.]
12. ACIM, I, page 592. [T-30. V. 8;1-2. page 637.]
13. ACIM, I, page 253. [T-14. II. 3;3-9. pages 272-273.]

CHAPTER FIVE
FEAR IS NOT A REALITY

1. ACIM, I, page 364. [T-18. VIII. 1;6-7 and 2;2. page 390.]

2. ACIM, I, page 443. [T-22. III. 6;5-8. page 476.]
3. ACIM, II, page 239. [W-133. page 245.]
4. ACIM, I, page 502. [T-25. IX. 4;4-6. page 539.]
5. Excerpts from the following speeches of Abraham Lincoln: address before the Young Men's Lyceum, Springfield, Illinois, January 27, 1838; eulogy to Henry Clay, Springfield, Illinois, July 6, 1852; address at Cooper Institute, New York City, February 27, 1860.
6. ACIM, II, page 277. [W-153. page 284.]
7. Matthew 6:10.
8. Matthew 5:39.
9. Luke 23:34.
10. ACIM, II, pages 247-248. [W-135. 17;1 and 19;2. pages 254-255.]
11. ACIM, II, page 287. [W-156. 4;1-4 and 6;1-2. page 294.]
12. ACIM, I, page 404. [T-20. IV. 8;5-12. page 434.]
13. ACIM, I, page 549. [T-28. I. 13;1-3. page 592.]
14. The Indian poet Mohammed Iqubal (1875-1938) wrote in the Urdu and Persian languages. (Editor)

CHAPTER SIX
INDIVIDUALITY

1. ACIM, II, page 233. [W-131. page 239.]
2. See Genesis 32:24-32.
3. ACIM, II, page 235. [W-131. 15;6. page 241.]

CHAPTER SEVEN
ULTIMATELY WE HAVE TO CONQUER FEAR

1. ACIM, II, page 360. [W-194. page 370.]
2. ACIM, II, page 36. [W-24. page 36.]
3. ACIM, II, page 79. [W-50. page 79.]
4. ACIM, II, page 171. [W-97. 7;2. page 173.]
5. ACIM, II, page 25. [W-15. page 25.]
6. ACIM, II, page 193. [W-109. 2;4. page 197.]
7. ACIM, I, pages 24-27. [T-2. VI. pages 28-31.]
8. Ibid. [T-2. VI. 8;5-9 and 9;1-14. pages 30-31.]

CHAPTER EIGHT
THE NEED TO STEP OUT OF THOUGHT

1. ACIM, III, page 81. [M-4. 1;1-2. page 85.]
2. ACIM, II, page 403. [W-Part II. 3. 1;1. page 413.]
3. ACIM, III, page 4. [M-2. 3;1. page 5.]
4. ACIM, II, page 466. [W-346. page 476.]
5. ACIM, II, page 16. [W-10. page 16.]
6. ACIM, II, page 77. [W-48. page 77.]
7. ACIM, II, page 466. [W-346. 1;1-7 and 2;1-2. page 476.]

CHAPTER NINE
THOUGHT IS INSANITY

1. ACIM, II, page 32. [W-21. page 32.]
2. ACIM, I, page 24. [T-2. V. 18;6. page 28.]
3. ACIM, II, page 162. [W-94. page 164.]
4. ACIM, II, page 193. [W-109. page 197.]
5. ACIM, II, page 162. [W-94. page 164.]

CHAPTER TEN
THE PRESSURES ON MANKIND

1. ACIM, I, page 281. [T-15. I. 8;2-5. pages 302-303.]

CHAPTER ELEVEN
"I CAN BE HURT BY NOTHING BUT MY THOUGHTS"

1. ACIM, II, page 428. [W-281. page 438.]
2. ACIM, III, page 8. [M-4. I. 1;4-7. page 9.]
3. Refers to Luke 8:11-12, Mark 13:11, and Matthew 10:19.
4. Refers to Matthew 6:34.
5. ACIM, II, page 79. [W-50. page 79.]
6. Refers to Lesson 65, ACIM, II, page 107. [W-65. page 108.]
7. ACIM, II, page 307. [W-165. 7;3-4 and 8;1-5. page 314.]
8. ACIM, II, page 428. [W-281. page 438.]
9. Matthew 5:40.
10. See: References, Introduction, no.26.
11. ACIM, III, page 21. [M-7. 4;6. page 22.]

CHAPTER TWELVE
"I AM UNDER NO LAWS BUT GOD'S"

1. ACIM, II, page 132. [W-76. page 134.]
2. ACIM, II, page 3. [W-1. page 3.]
3. ACIM, II, page 5. [W-3. page 5.]
4. ACIM, II, page 11. [W-7. page 11.]
5. ACIM, II, page 16. [W-10. page 16.]
6. ACIM, II, page 11. [W-7. page 11.]
7. ACIM, II, page 13. [W-8. page 13.]
8. ACIM, II, page 16. [W-10. page 16.]
9. ACIM, I, page 130. [T-8. II. 4;4. page 140.]
10. ACIM, II, page 132. [W-76. 4;1-3. page 134.]
11. ACIM, I, page 416. [T-21. I. 4;1. page 446.]
12. ACIM, I, page 399. [T-20. III. 1;3. page 429.]
13. ACIM, II, page 101. [W-61. page 102.]
14. ACIM, II, page 56. [W-37. page 56.]
15. ACIM, II, page 52. [W-35. page 53.]
16. ACIM, II, pages 132-134. [W-76. 11;2-6 and 12;1-3. pages 135-136.]
17. ACIM, I, page 256. [T-14. III. 6;1. page 275.]
18. ACIM, II, page 77. [W-48. page 77.]
19. ACIM, II, page 162. [W-94. page 164.]
20. ACIM, I, page 326. See also: References, Chapter Four, no.7. [T-16. VII. 12;1-7. page 350.]
21. ACIM, I, page 74. [T-5. IV. 1;2. page 81.]

AUTOBIOGRAPHY OF TARA SINGH

1. See: References, Introduction, no. 22.
2. ACIM, II, page 239. [W-133. page 245.]
3. ACIM, II, page 123. [W-72. 9;6. page 125.]
4. ACIM, II, page 471. [W-353. 1;3. page 481.]
5. Refers to Matthew 18:20.
6. ACIM, I, page 326. See also: References, Chapter Four, no. 7. [T-16. VII. 12;1-7. page 350.]
7. ACIM, II, page 79. [W-50. page 79.]
8. Refers to Joseph in the Old Testament. See Genesis 37 and following.

• *"NOTHING REAL CAN BE THREATENED"*

PURPOSE OF THE FOUNDATION FOR LIFE ACTION

1. See ACIM, I, pages 426-427; II, page 120 and following. [T-21. V. 5;1-11 and 6;1-6. page 457.] Also [W-71. page 121.]
2. ACIM, II, page 79. [W-50. page 79.]
3. ACIM, II, page 107. [W-65. page 108.]
4. ACIM, II, page 132. [W-76. page 134.]
5. Matthew 6:33.

STATEMENT OF THE PARTICIPANTS
OF THE ONE YEAR NON-COMMERCIALIZED RETREAT

1. ACIM, II, page 53. [W-35. page 53.]

Other Materials by Tara Singh Related To *A Course In Miracles*

BOOKS

A Gift for All Mankind
The Future of Mankind
How to Learn from A Course In Miracles
Commentaries on A Course In Miracles
Dialogues on A Course In Miracles
How to Raise a Child of God
Awakening a Child from Within
"Love Holds No Grievances" – The Ending of Attack
Remembering God in Everything You See
Moments Outside of Time
"What Is The Christ?"

AUDIOCASSETTES

Transforming Your Life with A Course In Miracles
True Meditation – A Practical Approach
Is It Possible to Rest the Brain?
Awakening the Light of the Mind
Keep the Bowl Empty
"What Is The Christ?"
Discovering Your Life's Work
All Relationships Must End in Love
Conflict Ends with Me
Undoing Self-Deception
The Heart of Forgiveness
Relationship with a True Teacher

What is A Course In Miracles?
A Course In Miracles Explorations
"Creation's Gentleness is All I See"
Making A Course In Miracles Work for You
Bringing A Course In Miracles into Application
Service — Finding Something of Your Own to Give

AUDIOCASSETTE COLLECTIONS

Audiocassette collections from Life Action Press offer a wealth of profound insights into personal transformation. Whatever your spiritual path, Tara Singh's powerful sharings will enrich your life and hasten your awakening.

ONE YEAR GIVEN TO GOD —
THE ONE YEAR NON-COMMERCIALIZED RETREAT

These brilliant sessions illumine many topics including creation, holy beings, yoga, the silent mind, integrity, forgiveness, and — not least — how to realize the truth of *A Course In Miracles*. A year's finest moments are captured on seventy-two 90-minute cassettes.

HOLDING HANDS WITH YOU —
EXPLORING THE DAILY LESSON OF THE COURSE

Tara Singh demonstrates the attention and reverence needed to make your own discoveries as you read *A Course In Miracles*. His comments on Lessons 1 to 50 help you to stay with the *Workbook* practice and realize the serene awareness the *Course* came to impart. Twenty-five helpful cassettes.

EXPLORING THE MANUAL FOR TEACHERS

A must for dedicated students of *A Course In Miracles*, this series sheds light on the role and character of the true teacher. Tara Singh brings his vast background, discrimination, and wisdom to reading the important third volume of the *Course*. A ten-cassette collection.

WAKE UP AND LISTEN — DAILY MEDITATIONS

Start your day uplifted by Tara Singh's clarity. Hear a fresh perspective on friendship, productivity, relationship, intrinsic work, ending judgment, and being of real service, among other themes. Each message is five to ten minutes long — enough to make space inside for a deeper contact with the Truth in you. Seventy messages on 10 cassettes.

SEVEN HOLY BEINGS

Tara Singh illustrates the qualities that make for greatness in the lives and teachings of some of the eternal beings that have deeply affected him: Jesus, Lord Buddha, Guru Nanak, Sri Sarada Devi (The Holy Mother), Swami Vivekananda, and Saraswati (The Goddess of Music). A unique seven-tape set.

VIDEOCASSETTE COLLECTION

SERVICE WITHOUT SACRIFICE

Tara Singh brilliantly defines the subtle relationship and balance between brain, mind, and body. He shows what it means to find your real function — far beyond the activities of survival or even "doing good." For each of us living in a society in crisis, these tapes are timely and essential. A set of six videocassettes.

VIDEOCASSETTES

The Power of Attention
How to Raise a Child of God
"There Must be Another Way"
Transforming Your Life with A Course In Miracles
A Course In Miracles is not to be Learned, but to be Lived

Please write or call for a free catalog of books and tapes:
LIFE ACTION PRESS
P.O. Box 48932
Los Angeles, California 90048
800/367-2246
213/964-5444

"the energy of gratefulness"

250

*seeing beyond the appearance —
the flower would introduce you to
the perfection — — — 106*

RETREATS
AND WORKSHOPS

rightness — 117

ANNUAL EASTER
AND YOM KIPPUR RETREATS
WITH TARA SINGH

At two week-long retreats each year, Tara Singh meets with those of serious intent to share on *A Course In Miracles*. The Easter retreat is usually on the West Coast and the Fall retreat, at Yom Kippur, is usually on the East Coast. In addition, Mr. Singh has agreed to lead week-end workshops throughout the United States.

Join Tara Singh for a retreat or workshop. Bring questions about the *Course* or your life. Discover what it is to quiet the mind. Explore how to heal relationships, find your life's purpose, step out of pressure, and deepen your inner growth. Examine what it would be to give part of your life to service.

For more information on these retreats and workshops, call 213/933-5591 or write the Joseph Plan Foundation, P.O. Box 481194-B, Los Angeles, California 90048.

ABOUT THE AUTHOR

TARA SINGH is known as a teacher, author, poet and humanitarian. The early years of his life were spent in a small village in Punjab, India. From this sheltered environment, at the age of nine, he and his mother traveled via Europe to Panama to join his father who was in business there. While in Panama he attended school for two years. He returned to India at the age of eighteen. His search for Truth, inspired by the family saint, led him at age twenty-two to the Himalayas where he lived for four years as an ascetic. During this period he outgrew conventional religion. He discovered that a mind conditioned by religious or secular beliefs is always limited.

In his next phase of growth, he responded to the poverty of India through participation in that country's postwar industrialization and international affairs. He became an associate of Mahatma Gandhi and a close friend of Prime Minister Nehru and Eleanor Roosevelt.

It was in the 1950's, as he outgrew his involvement with political and economic systems, that Mr. Singh was inspired by his association with Mr. J. Krishnamurti and the teacher of the Dalai Lama. He discovered that humanity's problems cannot be solved externally. Subsequently, he became more and more removed from worldly affairs and devoted several years of his life to the study and practice of yoga. The discipline imparted through yoga helped make possible a three-year period of silent retreat in Carmel, California in the early 1970's.

As he emerged from the years of silence in 1976, he came into contact with *A Course In Miracles*. Its impact on him was profound. He recognized its unique contribution as a scripture and saw it as the answer to man's urgent need for direct contact with Truth. There followed a close relationship with its Scribe, Dr. Helen Schucman. The *Course* has been the focal point of his life ever since. Mr. Singh recognizes and presents the *Course* as the Thoughts of God, and correlates it with the great spiritual teachings and religions of the world.

From Easter 1983 to Easter 1984, Mr. Singh conducted the One Year Non-Commercialized Retreat: A Serious Study of *A Course In Miracles*. It was an unprecedented, in-depth exploration of the *Course* under the sponsorship of the Foundation for Life Action. No tuition was charged. Since then, Mr. Singh has worked on a one-to-one basis with a small group of serious students.

In 1993, Mr. Singh established the Joseph Plan Foundation, a non-profit educational and charitable foundation organized to meet the primary needs of man and to introduce people to the joy of service.

the illusion of "becoming"

138

143

Additional copies of *Nothing Real Can Be Threatened* may be obtained by sending a check, money order, Discover, MasterCard or VISA number and expiration date to:

LIFE ACTION PRESS
P.O. Box 48932
Los Angeles, CA 90048
800/367-2246
213/964-5444

Softcover $13.95
        Add $3.00 shipping/handling.

A Course In Miracles may be ordered from
Life Action Press:

Three volume, hardcover edition $40.00

Combined, hardcover edition $30.00

Combined, hardcover **Spanish** edition $30.00

Combined, softcover edition $25.00

        Add $4.00 shipping/handling.

A Course In Miracles may also be ordered from
the publisher, the Foundation for Inner Peace,
P.O. Box 1104, Glen Ellen, CA 95442.
707/939-0200

California residents please add 7.25% sales tax.
Los Angeles County, California residents add
8.25% sales tax.

Thank you.